The Ultimate Guide to Wild Canines, Primitive Dogs, and Pariah Dogs

Marjorie Daley

LP Media Inc. Publishing

Text copyright © 2019 by LP Media Inc.

All rights reserved.

No part of this book may be reproduced or transmitted in any form or by any means, electronic or mechanical, including photocopying, recording, or by an information storage and retrieval system - except by a reviewer who may quote brief passages in a review to be printed in a magazine or newspaper - without permission in writing from the publisher. For information address LP Media Inc. Publishing, 3178 253rd Ave. NW, Isanti, MN 55040

www.lpmedia.org

Publication Data

Marjorie Daley

The Ultimate Guide to Wild Canines, Primitive Dogs, and Pariah Dogs ---- First edition.

Summary: "Successfully raising a Wild Canine, Primitive Dog, and Pariah Dog from puppy to old age" --- Provided by publisher.

ISBN: 978-1-07999-7-651

[1. Wild Canines, Primitive Dogs, and Pariah Dogs --- Non-Fiction] I. Title.

This book has been written with the published intent to provide accurate and authoritative information in regard to the subject matter included. While every reasonable precaution has been taken in preparation of this book the author and publisher expressly disclaim responsibility for any errors, omissions, or adverse effects arising from the use or application of the information contained inside. The techniques and suggestions are to be used at the reader's discretion and are not to be considered a substitute for professional veterinary care. If you suspect a medical problem with your dog, consult your veterinarian.

Design by Sorin Rădulescu

First paperback edition, 2019

Cover Photo Courtesy of Terri Martin

TABLE OF CONTENTS

ACKNOWLEDGEMENTS	9
WHY THIS BOOK	11
DAX THE CAROLINA DOG	12

CHAPTER 1
Wild Canines — 18
Clarifying Terminology	18
What Are Wild Canines?	19
Wolf and Wolf Dog	20
Coyote and Coydog	22
Coywolf	25
Australian Dingoes	25
The Short Version	27

CHAPTER 2
Primitive Dogs and Pariah Dogs — 28
What Are Primitive Dogs and Pariah Dogs?	28
Spitz-type Dogs	30
Primitive-type Dogs	32
Indian Pariah Dog	32
Xoloitzcuintli	34
Carolina Dog	37
Identified Breeds of Primitive Dogs	39
The Short Version	41

CHAPTER 3
Is a Wild Canine or Wild Canine Cross Right for You? — 42
Wild Canine Issues	42
Concerns to Consider Before You Bring Home a Cross	43
General Wild Dog Attitudes	44
Truth 1: They Are Highly Social and Live in a Tightly Bonded Pack	45
Truths 2 and 3: Their Pack Structure Is Defined and They May Challenge for Status	46

Truth 4: They Are Highly Territorial	47
Truth 5: They Have A High Prey Drive	47
Truth 6: They Are Extremely Alert	48
Truth 7: They Are Wary of Humans	49
Truth 8: They Become "Unpredictable"	49
Housing	49
Exercise	52
Training	52
Food	53
Medical Care	55
Safety	56
Homeowner's Insurance	56
Volkosobs	57
The Short Version	57

CHAPTER 4

Is a Primitive Dog Right for You? ... 58

The Dog de Jour (The Dog of the Day)	59
What to Consider Before Bringing Home a Primitive Dog	60
General Attitudes	62
Independent and Aloof (Tenacious)	62
Suspicious and Alert (Engaged)	63
Clever and Stubborn (Determined)	65
Sensitive (Empathetic and Honest)	65
Denning Behavior	66
Prey Drive	66
Housing	67
Exercise	67
Food	68
Training the Primitive	68
The Short Version	69

CHAPTER 5

Acquiring Your Dog ... 70

Adopting versus Buying	70
Finding a Reputable Rescue	71
Wolf Dog and Dingo Specific Rescues	73
Importing a Dog	75
Legally Owning a Wolf Dog, Coydog, or Dingo/DingoX	76
The Short Version	77

CHAPTER 6
Preparing Your Home for Your Wild Canine ... 78
Outside Issues ... 79
Current Pets and Livestock ... 81
Children ... 83
Training Classes ... 85
The Short Version ... 85

CHAPTER 7
Preparing Your Home for Your Primitive Dog ... 86
Outside Issues ... 87
Current Pets and Livestock ... 87
Children ... 90
Training Classes ... 91
The Short Version ... 91

CHAPTER 8
Living with the Wild Canine or Primitive Dog ... 92
Standing by Your Expectations ... 92
What Is Socialization? ... 94
Socializing a Puppy ... 94
Socializing an Adult ... 95
What Is Bad Behavior in Dogs? ... 95
Boredom ... 97
Lack of Exercise ... 97
Lack of Socialization ... 98
Genetics ... 99
Illness and Injury ... 99
Inconsistent Home Life ... 99
Fear ... 100
How to Properly Correct Your Wild Canine or Primitive Dog ... 101
How to Crate Train ... 102
Chewing ... 103
Growling and Barking ... 104
Aggression ... 105
Digging ... 105
Separation Anxiety ... 107
Running Away ... 107
The Short Version ... 107

CHAPTER 9
Traveling with Wild Canines and Primitives **108**
Kenneling **109**
Flying **109**
Hotel Stays **112**
Crossing State or International Boundaries **112**
The Short Version **113**

THE FINAL HOWL

APPENDIX 1
United States **118**

APPENDIX 2
Canada **132**

APPENDIX 3
Australia **135**

ACKNOWLEDGEMENTS

The works cited for this book ran to 21 pages. Since publishing the complete list would be prohibitive, I'd like to single out the people who generously donated time and effort to give me personal insights, proof reading, and experiences.

Beta and Proofreaders:
- Madora Daley-Green
- Robin Poseyblue
- Robin Daley
- Jennie Lawrence

Ideas:
- Betsy Moore
- Jennifer Holroyd

Interviews and Information:
- J Worth McAlister (North Carolina Wildlife Resources Commission)
- Susan Weidel (W.O.L.F. Sanctuary)
- Sydney Brooke Cooper
- Irina Weese DVM PhD
- and Mike and Cindy Boyd
- Sandy Myers (Rockin E Dog Training)
- Blair Barta (Manitoba Wildlife and Fisheries Branch)
- Colen, B. (Missouri Dept. of Conservation)
- Ryan Wentzel
- Jenny Young
- Darlene Kobobel (Colorado Wolf and Wildlife Center)
- Rick Hamrick (Mississippi Dept Wildlife, Fisheries, and Parks)
- Leighann Harnett DVM (Shubenacadie Wildlife Park, Nova Scotia)

- Marianne Hudson (Alabama Department of Conservation & Natural Resources)
- Captain Walter Cook (Tennessee Wildlife Resources Agency)
- British Columbia Helpdesk – Carolyn S
- Cory Ludeman
- Amanda Kamps (Wisconsin Department of Natural Resources)
- Penelope Inan
- Alisia OroBello
- Nicole Strauss
- Lisa Rhoades Jett
- Michael Hall
- Jennie Lawrence
- Kayla Marie Kolberg
- Giovanna Suedan Quintero
- Phillip Kilbreath (Montana Fish, Wildlife & Parks)
- Vida Mae Lantz (Nova Scotia Lands and Forestry)
- Mark McKinnon (Georgia Department of Natural Resources)
- Tasmania Department of Primary Industries, Parks, Water and Environment – Naomi
- Will Newberry (Alaska Department of Fish and Game)
- Linnea Petercheff (Indiana Division of Fish and Wildlife)
- Scott Snyder (Florida Wildlife Commission)
- Tracey Spencer (Maryland Department of Natural Resources)
- Jessica Wolff (Nevada Department of Natural Resources)
- Tara Karleen
- Brad Compton, Region 3 Supervisor, Idaho Department of Fish and Game

WHY THIS BOOK

The Ultimate Guide to Wild Canines, Primitive Dogs, and Pariah Dogs is geared toward the experienced dog owner who wants to own a pure wild canine, a wolf dog, coydog, dingoX, or primitive/pariah dog. In this book we will examine pureblood wild canines and their crosses and look at several primitive/pariah breeds. We will lay out the challenges that you can expect from these breeds, including housing, transporting, and socializing. We will also discuss the current state and provincial laws surrounding ownership of wild canines.

This is not a training manual. If you are an inexperienced dog owner and think having a wild canine or cross is cool or a status symbol, please read this book very carefully. Wild canines are not for the inexperienced dog owner. For the sake of the dog you plan to bring home, please consider your decision very carefully. These dogs are a challenge even for experienced dog handlers. Wild animals and their crossbreeds do not belong in 99% of homes. The rehoming options are slim, and your pet wild canine may end up paying for your decision with its life.

Primitive dogs have a long history of living on the edges of human habitation. They may not come with the same legal challenges as a wild canine, but you will still have plenty of work ahead of you including training and socializing your primitive. Carefully think through your decision to adopt a primitive. Bringing home a "couch wolf" can cause problems in your home.

If you've accidentally gotten a primitive dog from a shelter, I highly encourage you to read this book, then find a reputable trainer who understands that this is not just a dog. I acquired my primitive dog accidentally and while I was an experienced dog owner, I was still baffled until I realized what she was and adapted to her behaviors.

A common domesticated dog is a huge responsibility. However, a wild or primitive dog requires far more work. Owning one may be the greatest experience in your life, but it will also be one of the biggest challenges.

For the sake of your future pet, take the time to read this book carefully.

DAX THE CAROLINA DOG

Photo Courtesy of Marjorie Daley

Back in 1998, my family and I went to the Birmingham Animal Shelter, looking for a half-shepherd half-Lab puppy. I liked Labs, my husband like shepherds. We were very pleased when we found a puppy with floppy Lab ears and shepherd coloring, labeled as a Lab-shepherd cross. Unbeknownst to us and to the shelter, we were not taking home a water-loving, ball-fetching domestic dog. Instead, we were taking home a puzzle with a bunch of pieces mislabeled. It took us a long time and many mistakes to figure out the puzzle and get the pieces in the right places. Along the way, we discovered that life with what turned out to be a primitive dog was an adventure, a challenge, a series of what-now moments, and some errors. Hopefully, at the end of this book, you'll understand a bit more about primitives and avoid the mistakes we made.

All we knew about our new dog was that Dax had been found trotting down a dirt road in Nowhere, Alabama. She was maybe five weeks old. When we met her at the shelter, she was skittish but made it very clear by crying and pawing at her cage when our backs were turned that she wanted to come home with us. But if we turned to look at her, she cowered. There was just something about her eyes and the fact that she wanted us that made us keep coming back to her cage. We spent some time with her in a meet and greet room and eventually, she quit being afraid of us and started interacting.

On the ride home, she sat proudly on my lap, wet from her recent flea bath and still crawling with fleas. We noticed she had two white forepaws. We called these her white gloves, because she was so very dignified – very much a southern lady.

The unexpected behaviors started the moment Dax arrived in our home. For the first few weeks, the only items she would eat voluntarily were acorns and cockroaches. In order to feed her, I sat with her and fed her one piece of kibble at a time. For the next eight years, we had to keep her food in a secluded place if we wanted her to eat. Otherwise, walking past her would frighten her away for several hours. In her older years, she allowed us to put her food in the kitchen, but we had to avoid looking at her when she was eating. Otherwise, she would immediately walk away.

Another food oddity was that Dax would not touch any food within her reach. She even refused to eat dropped food until given permission. This was not taught; it was completely her decision. We could leave anything – even her favorite pizza – at nose height and walk away for hours. It would still be there until we specifically gave her permission to take it.

Another oddity was her insistence on being with me. I was suffering from depression and Dax was to be part of my recovery. Somehow, she knew how fragile I was. The first night, we tucked our tired little puppy into her crate and then spent the next four hours listening to her cry. I finally gave up and moved her bed to the floor beside our bed. For the rest of her life, she slept where she could wake me up from PTSD-induced nightmares or offer a cold nose when I cried. She also determined the household schedule. I got up when she thought I should and went to bed when she demanded I did. She expected me to accompany her outside and made it very clear that I was going to exercise with her.

Dax was also the most stubborn creature I had ever worked with. My animal experience included working with hot- and warm-blooded horses, dogs, cats, an owl, and a mountain lion. Even so, Dax could make me so frustrated. In desperation, I signed up for puppy classes. I spent two to three hours a day training her, but I discovered that she would train for no more than ten minutes at a time, and a lot of variety was necessary. We tried agility. She loved it. But she would do every obstacle once, and then she was finished for the day. Retrieving a ball? Her attitude was that I threw it, so I should go get it.

Dax was almost impossible to housetrain. It took months. I had never had such a hard dog to housebreak. Most of my old dogs seemed to figure it out immediately. This one... I finally attached her to my belt loop with a six-foot leash. Since she was stuck with me, I could monitor her every move and take her immediately outside with lots of praise and treats. Once she grasped the idea, she never had another accident until the very end of her life.

She was also incredibly dignified and solemn. Even as a tiny pup, she never was giddy or silly. She was a wise old soul in a puppy body, absolutely hated to be laughed at, and would stalk off to sulk if she felt she was mocked.

For being half Lab (so we thought), she hated water. Eventually, she would swim, but always with an air that she was just being agreeable. Fortunately, Dax did not smell. No doggy stinky foot pads, no sour dog smell. Nothing. On the rare occasions that she was kenneled, she would come out with the stink of dog kennel on her fur. All it took was a ten-minute hike and the smell was gone.

Dax hunted like a fox, leaping into the air and catching mice underfoot. She was death on four legs. Her obsession was squirrels and chipmunks because she never managed to catch either.

Another odd behavior was digging nose-sized holes all over the yard only so she could put her nose into each hole and snort.

Dax had severe claustrophobia – possibly her only anxiety. I always assumed that she had been the lone survivor of a family den cave-in. She would dig shallow burrows, but never anything where she was underground.

Dax adored babies and was thrilled when we brought home first our daughter and then our son. She spent hours watching them from her vantage point on the couch. Any noise was immediately investigated. If they cried, she would be very worried and try to make them feel better. However, if they were in trouble, she refused to comfort them, instead moving away. She was an Aunty dog, and she took that role very seriously.

Gradually, we realized this was no half-Lab half-shepherd mutt. This dog was unique in her behaviors and her outlook on the world. The closest I could come to her looks and attitude was a Canaan dog or maybe a Finnish Spitz. However, the odds of either breed in Alabama having puppies and abandoning them on a rural road was just not working for me.

And then the *Smithsonian* magazine came, about a year after Dax arrived in our home. And in the article on Carolina Dogs was a photograph of my dog, or at least her nearest cousin. It was then we realized exactly what she was. A primitive dog. A dog without human interference. A dog who was not domesticated. All her behaviors suddenly became clear.

In those pre-internet days, I spent a lot of time writing letters to Carolina Dog experts and learning what I could from interlibrary loan. Most peo-

Dax the Carolina Dog

Photo Courtesy of Marjorie Daley

Photo Courtesy of Marjorie Daley

ple pooh-poohed the idea of a wild dog breed that had survived centuries of neglect and diluted blood lines. Dog snobs said she was a mongrel; the end result of many generations of random dog mixings. But watching her operate made it very clear that she was no mutt. She was different. Stubborn, opinionated, dignified, gracious, with a very defined pack structure and expectations for the rest of her pack.

Eventually, we decided to bring in another puppy. Unfortunately, it was a disaster. Had we known then what we know now about Carolina Dogs, we would never have attempted to add another dog into the mix. Our puppy turned out much larger and stronger than Dax and after the new dog made two attempts to kill Dax, we went to a professional for help. The new puppy, unbeknownst to us, was a dog fighting ring bait puppy and was mentally damaged. We were unable to rehome the pup and unwilling to have her euthanized. As a result, our house was divided in half using gates. If one dog was outside, the other had to wait. If both dogs were in the car, the bait puppy had to wear a muzzle. This went on for six very long years.

At fourteen years of age, Dax suffered a mild stroke. After that, she lost her will to hike. She went, because she had always gone, but her joy was gone. After I spent a few cold, snowy evenings finding her and carrying her back in the house because she had hidden away outside to die, we gathered together and euthanized her.

Of all the dogs I had before Dax and all the ones after, no other has been able to match her stubbornness, sensitivity, sheer intelligence, wicked sense of humor, integrity, or the joy she brought to our lives.

Without Dax, this book would not have been possible for me. The hands-on experience of living with a primitive dog was the beginning of writing this book. As I contacted other primitive dog owners for their experiences, we were amazed at how similar our stories were, even if the breeds were from different parts of the world. Hopefully, this book will help you understand how special primitive dogs are and how to live successfully with them.

CHAPTER 1
Wild Canines

I woke up one morning thinking about wolves and realized that wolf packs function as families. Everyone has a role, and if you act within the parameters of your role, the whole pack succeeds, and when that falls apart, so does the pack.

Jodi Picoult, author

Clarifying Terminology

A bit of terminology before we begin. The term "hybrid" is commonly used to describe the offspring of a wild canine and a domesticated dog. That terminology is not correct. A hybrid is a cross that results in a generally sterile offspring, like mules (horse/donkey) or ligers (lion/tiger). I say generally because, very rarely, a hybrid will be fertile. The offspring of wild canines and domestic dogs are fertile. Since they are not hybrids, I will refer to them by the more correct term of cross.

Crosses may be low-, mid-, or high-content crosses. The higher the content, the more wild canine genes the offspring will have.

Photo Courtesy of Michelle Proulx
W.O.L.F. Sanctuary, Colorado

What Are Wild Canines?

Wild canids and canines are found the world over, in every ecosystem and climate from the arctic to the very tip of Africa and South America. The genus *Canis* includes all "true dogs" like coyotes (*Canis latrans*), jackals (*Canis sp*), wolves (*Canis lupus*), and the subsets of domestic dogs (*Canis familiaris*) and dingoes (*Canis dingo*). I am using the term wild canine instead of wild dog throughout this book because it is more correct. Using the term "dog" to refer to a coyote, wolf, or dingo brings with it the impression that these animals are dogs and have doggy personalities and attitudes. To be clear: wild canines are not dogs, they are dog cousins.

Photo Courtesy of Jason Stockmyer

All other wild canids are not true canines. These distant relatives include foxes, dholes, bush dogs, maned wolves, and African Hunting Dogs. Since none of these except foxes are legal to import or own, and are not actually canines in anything but appearance, they are truly wild animals, generally un-domesticable, and are not suitable as pets. According to Captain Walter Cook of the Tennessee Wildlife Resources Agency, many foxes are abandoned because of their stench and are not recommended as pets.

The wild canines we'll focus on are coyotes, wolves, and dingoes. They are animals that have never been domesticated, except dingoes, and have lived without human contact. Wild canines may also be the generation F1 or offspring of one pure wild canine parent and one domestic dog parent (50% wolf) or F2 that includes one F1 parent and one domestic dog parent (25% wolf). Keep in mind that the higher content in terms of "wild genes," the more a cross will act like their wilder ancestor. All wild canines share some unique behaviors such as coming into heat once a year, setting up and defending territories, communal nursing, and food regurgitation.

We'll look at each wild canine in detail and define how they behave and interact within a pack structure.

Wolf and Wolf Dog

Photo Courtesy of Michelle Proulx
W.O.L.F. Sanctuary, Colorado

Wolves are part of European mythology, from eaters of little girls to monsters that turn from human to wolf under a full moon. They inspire awe and fear, and in the western US and Canada, they are quite possibly the most hated wild animal. Wolves are continually at the center of massive court battles. To some Westerners they are the epitome of the true wild and for others, they are vicious livestock killers. The truth lies somewhere in between.

There are two defined species of wolves, red wolves (*Canis rufus*) and gray wolves (*Canis lupus*). Scientists have discovered a third wolf family candidate, an Ethiopian canine (*Canis simensis*), which may or may not be a true wolf; the data is still out.

Red wolves are an endangered species found only in the southeastern United States. Regulated by the United States Fish and Wildlife Service (USFW), they are a protected species. Ownership is strictly forbidden. One subspecies of gray wolf, the Mexican Gray (*Canis lupus baileyi*), is considered imperiled but "non-essential" and thus is denied protection by the USFW.

Gray wolves are found across the northern hemisphere including the US and Canada, Latin America, Western and Eastern Europe, the Middle East, and Asia. Experts debate how many subspecies there are, but we will not look at specific subspecies for this book. For the purpose of this book, subspecies do not really matter. Wolves are wolves!

Their diverse habitats, from tundra to desert, account for the variation in coloration from white in the northern most snowy latitudes to black in more heavily timbered regions. Gray is probably the most common color.

Wolves are the largest members of the canine family, commonly four to six and a half feet long, 40 to 175 pounds, and twenty-six to thirty-nine inches at the shoulder. In comparison to a common domesticated dog, wolves are generally taller than Great Danes. Most people are familiar with Labrador-sized dogs. A wolf is taller by between three to fifteen inches and heavier by up to one hundred pounds.

Chapter 1 Wild Canines

Wolves are social animals who live in packs structured around an alpha male and female. Alphas, the pack leaders, are generally the only breeding pair and are often, but not always, the best hunters in the pack. The rest of the pack consists of family members and, rarely, a dispersed wolf from another pack. The alphas set the rules. The rest of the wolves organize themselves within the family. Since the primary goal of the wolf pack is to raise pups, the other wolves may be babysitters or assist in hunts. Wolves consider you part of their pack or not part of the pack. They do not accept new people, animals, or other wolves readily.

> **HELPFUL TIP**
> **Laws About Wild Canines**
>
> Wild canines like dingoes, coyotes, wolf and their crosses may be illegal to own or require special permits in many places. Make sure you understand your local laws about owning wild or exotic pets before bringing home a wild canine.

Wolf pups under the age of two years generally do not have a rank. At age two, they begin to find their place within the pack and especially with age mates. Any status issues occur when there is an opening or a weakness in one of the sub-wolves. Often the wolves with the strongest personalities, not physical prowess, rise to the top of the hierarchy. Loss of one of the alphas generally ends in the pack dispersing, not in another rising to the top.

Highly territorial, wolves actively patrol and defend their territory against intruders. In fact, in Yellowstone National Park, most wolf mortality comes from inter-pack fights over territory.

Wolves are very vocal and whine, growl, howl, and occasionally bark. They are extremely aware of everything that happens in their territory and need to check out the sound, smell, or sight of something different.

Wolf dogs are part wolf and part dog, generally bred by humans. Most are descended from gray wolves and will retain many of their wild characteristics. Voluntary breeding may take place if there is no other option for the wolf, but that is extremely uncommon. Regulation for wolf dogs is very patchwork and left to the state/province or local ordinances. Always check your state/provincial laws before bringing home a wolf dog.

Many dogs advertised as wolf dogs are not truly wolf dogs but are bred from malamute-type and German shepherd–type dogs. The results look enough like a wolf to fool most people, and they bring in a lot of revenue to the breeders. However, if an animal is represented as a wolf dog, whether or not it actually is, then it is also regulated as a wolf dog.

Coyote and Coydog

Coyotes range between thirty-two and thirty-seven inches long, twenty-one to twenty-six to at the shoulder and twenty to fifty pounds. Comparatively, coyotes are smaller both height- and weight-wise than the average Labrador Retriever. Coyotes range from gray to reddish brown and may have a whitish throat, chest, and/or belly.

Eastern Canadian coyotes tend to be slightly larger because they may interbreed with wolves. Eastern coyotes tend to weigh between thirty and fifty pounds and have a nose to tail length between forty-eight and sixty inches. Their legs are longer than a western coyote's. According to wildlife officials in the southern United States, coyotes may breed with red wolves. The offspring appear more like red wolves than coyotes and are regulated as such.

Coyotes are mostly loners, though they do live in temporarily bonded pairs to raise a litter. They generally hunt in pairs and occasionally hunt in packs. If you are lucky, you may hear a family or temporary pack singing.

Coyotes have a home range (generally a subdivision of the territorial range) that is the same size as their territory. Coyotes defend their territories from intruders. They, like wolves, are very aware of any changes to their surroundings. They are also incredibly wary of humans and can become neurotic when caged or contained.

They also tend to constantly evaluate potential prey for weaknesses, and because they are opportunistic hunters, practically everything is potential prey. They are fairly noisy, with vocalizations ranging from howls to barks, yips to growls, and whines to whimpers. Coyotes also "gape" and hiss when frightened. A gape involves a defensive body posture and wide-open mouth that resembles a cat arching its back in fear.

Coydogs are coyote-dog crosses. Though coyotes and dogs may breed voluntarily more frequently than wolf-dog crosses, it is still extremely uncommon. Coyotes have a well-deserved reputation for killing dogs, rather than mating with them, but hormones can overcome that instinct. Knowledgeable dog trainers estimate that it takes several generations of interbreeding for a coydog to become less wary than its coyote parents and grandparents.

Coydogs generally have more coyote behaviors than dog behaviors, and their general attitudes often depend on what type of dog is represented in their dog side. Socialization early and often is extremely important with all coydogs. Most are very much one-person dogs and do best in a one-dog household. Like coyotes, they may gape in fear and hiss. Coydogs like to explore and are escape artists who can become very destructive. Like all wild and primitive dogs, coydogs are not good first-time dogs.

Chapter 1   Wild Canines

While coyotes are generally illegal to own, coydogs ownership varies widely. Laws can be unclear, so take some time to look up your state's laws and/or discuss them with a professional like your animal control officer or game warden. Most coydogs, unless they look like a coyote, are legally considered dogs. If you purchase or otherwise acquire a known coydog, no matter how it looks, you may be in violation of your state's laws.

Coywolf

Coywolves are a cross between a wolf and a coyote. Their very existence is in scientific doubt and argued over regularly. If these really are crosses, they tend to occur in the wild and are extremely rare. Genetic testing of coyotes in the eastern US and Canada shows a mix of mostly coyote with a bit of wolf and dog genes added in. This is because an animal in heat will choose to mate with what is available.

Purported coywolves are larger than the average coyote and can hunt larger prey. They also bring with them both aspects of coyote and wolf behavior.

Australian Dingoes

Australian dingoes (*Canis lupus dingo*) are wild canines found in Australia. Based on the scientific name, dingoes are considered a subspecies of wolves. Others claim that they are separate from wolves or a distinct subspecies of domestic dogs (*Canis dingo* and *Canis familiaris dingo* respectively). Regardless where dingoes fit into the canine family tree, the Australian dingo is unique.

Photo Courtesy of Bianca and Thomas Walker

The dingo is the only canine found in Australia prior to European immigration. Archaeological evidence places dingoes in Australia about 3,500 years ago. However, DNA evidence suggests

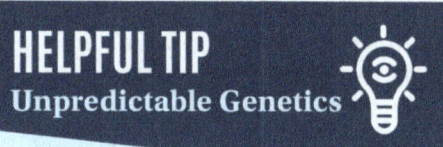

HELPFUL TIP
Unpredictable Genetics

Wolf dog breeders will convince you that a dog with one wolf parent (F1) and one half wolf and half dog parent (F2) is exactly 75% wolf and will act like 75% wolf. That's not how genetics works. Your cross could end up with much more or less genetic material than that from its wolf lineage. There is no way to know for sure how many wolf traits a cross will display.

that dingoes may have been in Australia far longer, possibly as far back as 18,000 years ago.

The best evidence suggests that the ancestors of the Aboriginals brought dingoes as domesticated dogs from (relatively) nearby islands. The dingo's closest genetic relative is the New Guinea Singing Dog, found on the islands thought to be the departure point for aboriginal immigration to Australia. Once dingoes arrived in Australia, they abandoned their human companions and went feral and then became wild.

A feral animal is one who either recently escaped from domesticity or is descended from domestic ancestors. A wild animal is one that has had no human interaction or interference. Dingoes are considered wild because of the sheer length of time between living with humans and today.

Dingoes feature prominently in Aboriginal spiritual and cultural practices, with the interactions over the millennia memorialized in cave paintings, rock carvings, dreamtime stories, and ceremonies. They are found throughout Australia, except for Tasmania. They live in a wide variety of habitats – deserts, rainforests, mountains, and grasslands. More remote areas tend to have purer dingo populations.

In the late 1880s, Australian settlers erected a 3,488-mile long fence to stop the spread of rabbits. In the early 1900s, this fence was modified to keep dingoes away from sheep and is now known as the Dingo Fence. Dingoes on the southeastern side of the fence were eradicated. However, the fence has not proved to be impermeable, and dingoes have made their way through it. Inconsistently, the two contiguous states, New South Wales and Victoria, that are fully enclosed by the Dingo Fence have allowed ownership of dingoes.

A dingo is usually sandy to reddish colored, about twenty to twenty-four inches tall, and weighs between twenty-two and forty-four pounds, again smaller than the average Labrador.

Dingoes live within clearly defined territories in packs of about ten to twelve members. They have a hierarchical structural similar to wolves, with an alpha male and female. The Dingo Den, a dingo rescue, describes wild dingoes as Australia's equivalent to lions or tigers and recommends people have no contact with them. Rare dingo-human attacks aside, dingoes tend to be wary and run from threats.

Dingoes may hunt alone or in packs, depending on their prey. As opportunistic hunters, animals that choose food based on availability rather than on preference, they have high prey drives. Animals ranging from kangaroos to lizards are fair prey. Dingoes are primarily carnivores and scavengers but will eat plants and fruits. The flexibility of their diet can be seen in behaviors of different dingoes from different areas. For instance, Frazier Island dingoes eat fish, and Northern Territory dingoes will hunt water buffalo.

As with all wild canines, dingoes breed once a year. In packs, the alpha female kills any pups other than her own. Dingoes do not bark, but howl much like wolves.

Dingoes and dogs interbreed readily in Australia, and many urban areas have populations of DingoX. Depending on your Australian state, you may or may not be able to own a dingo. You cannot legally import a dingo to the United States or Canada.

While some people use "dingo" to describe the American Carolina Dog or Australian cattle dog or heeler, this is incorrect. True dingoes are found only in Australia and are a specific species quite distinct from heelers.

The Short Version

- There are four true "wild canines," of which we've discussed three: wolves, coyotes, and dingoes.
- The canine family includes canines, foxes, and dog-like canines such as African Maned Wolves.
- Wolves are social animals who live in packs structured around an alpha male and female.
- Coyotes constantly evaluate potential prey for weaknesses and because they are opportunistic hunters, practically everything is potentially prey.
- Wild dingoes are Australia's equivalent to lions or tigers.

CHAPTER 2
Primitive Dogs and Pariah Dogs

Fall in love with a dog, and in many ways, you enter a new orbit, a universe that features not just new colors but new rituals, new rules, a new way of experiencing attachment.

Caroline Knapp, author

What Are Primitive Dogs and Pariah Dogs?

Primitive dogs come from ancient lineages and still have many of their wolf ancestor characteristics such as annual fertile periods and communal nursing. Primitives are classified as dog types or breeds that have always been linked to specific regions or countries. They have not interbred much with other dogs brought in primarily by Europeans.

Pariah dogs live on the outskirts of human settlements. These often have similar features to primitive dogs and may be feral (former pets or descended from former pets) or truly undomesticated. Pariahs often exhibit wolf-like behaviors such as coming into heat once a year, setting up and defending territories, communal nursing, and food regurgitation. For ease of terminology, we will refer to pariahs as primitives because they are so very similar to each other in behaviors. There are roughly fifty-five recognized primitive dogs breeds in the world.

Are these mongrels or true primitive dogs? With the advent of DNA testing, there is evidence that primitive dogs are unique and have different DNA than domestic dogs. Some primitives have been defined as breeds for thousands of years. In fact, several primitive breeds like Akitas and Shibas are the oldest docu-

HELPFUL TIP
Primitive Dogs vs Wild Canines

Primitive dogs may have many of the same features you're looking for in a wild canine, but they are more likely to be accepted in places where wild canines may not be (like the vet, groomer, or boarding facilities). This is an important factor to consider when you're deciding between a wild canine or cross and a primitive dog.

mented breeds in the world. Many current dog breeds are descended from "types" or dogs that naturally preferred to hunt, retrieve, or herd, for instance. In the 18th and 19th centuries, in Europe, these "types" were refined as dogs were formally bred for specific tasks and then recognized as breeds with breed standards. While a few primitives have this long association, most have traditionally just been considered mongrels.

If you are looking for "proof" that primitives are closer to what dogs looked like in the beginning of human/dog interaction, consider the Cuween dog skulls. Cuween Hill Cairn is in Firth on the Orkney Islands in Scotland.

Basenji

The cairn, dated to about 3,100 BCE (5,000 years ago), is made of a roofed chamber cut from solid bedrock and accessible only by a small tunnel.

Roughly 4,500 years ago, 24 dog skulls were interred in the cairn. These were rediscovered in the 19th century. Recently, scientists recreated one of the dog skulls using facial reconstruction techniques usually reserved for humans. With its erect ears, longer face, and larger brain space than most modern dogs, the skull resembles the skulls of many primitive dogs today. Because the cairn contained no skeletons, scientists cannot reconstruct the dogs' bodies, but the Cuween dog appears to be similar in size to a collie based on skull measurements.

HELPFUL TIP
Primitive Dogs versus Domestic Dogs

While primitive dogs and domestic dogs looks very much alike, primitive dogs are lived by their wits for far longer than domestic dogs. Primitive dogs revert to wolf-like behaviors when they are wild. Domestic dogs have been bred, for the most part, for servility and docility. Your primitive will be neither, but they can be well trained and well socialized with careful training.

All primitives have some very similar character traits – independent, suspicious, clever, aloof, sensitive, alert, and stubborn are commonly used to describe these dogs. They also have extremely high prey drives. Almost every primitive dog owner mentions that primitives do not smell, even when wet, or, at most, may have a popcorn odor.

Primitives are divided into two types, the Spitz-type, and the Primitive-type.

Spitz-type Dogs

Spitz-type dogs are found in the northern hemisphere, particularly in arctic regions. They have been associated with humans for thousands of years. As mentioned before, several Asian Spitz-types, like Shibas, are the most ancient established dog breeds. As any husky, malamute, or Shiba-inu owner will tell you, Spitz-types still have all the primitive character traits listed above.

Spitz-types have dense double coats, pricked ears, and curved or recurved tails. The dogs with less human-driven selective breeding tend to have curved tails. The recurve was created as a breed standard. Because Spitz-types have had a great deal of human interaction and selective breed-

CHAPTER 2   Primitive Dogs and Pariah Dogs

Shiba Inu

ing, they fall outside the scope of this book until they cross with wolves! Keep in mind that many of the "wolf dog" puppies being sold are actually nothing more than Spitz-type primitive dogs.

Primitive-type Dogs

Primitive-type dogs look very similar to Spitz-type, except that most have short, dense double coats suitable for living in hotter climates. Primitive dogs have accompanied humans for at least 15,000 years and one breed, now known as Canaan Dog, is mentioned in the Bible. Other common primitive-type breeds include Pharaoh Hounds, Basenjis, and Ridgebacks. These dogs, like primitives that have been in close contact with humans, have had more selective breeding.

Let's look at three primitive dogs including my favorite, Carolina Dogs.

Indian Pariah Dog

Indian Pariah Dogs, or INDogs, are found in India and are a common sight living around the garbage dumps. The dogs retain pricked ears, curved tails, and many behaviors common to primitives. There are several adoption agencies that bring INDogs to the US and Australia for adoption. INDog researchers describe them as very hardy, alert, independent, able to think independently, and perfectly adapted to the wild life or life with humans.

We will address import laws and considerations in Chapter 5: Acquiring Your Dog.

Interestingly, all Indian languages have a word that means "native dog." These include neri kukur in Bangladeshi, naatu naai in Tamil, and deshee kutta in Hindi. These words all refer to a dog with erect ears, short coat, and curved tail.

Many urban INDogs show evidence of crossbreeding with European dogs with traits such as floppy ears. Village INDogs far from populations with heavy European influence tend to be purer. These closely resemble ancient depictions recorded in traditional art and statuary.

INDogs tend to be 20 to 25 inches at the shoulder and weigh between 26 and 44 pounds. They are lean and muscular with coloration from light fawn to dark red-brown. They can have white markings. They have pricked ears and a curved tail. Floppy ears and colors other than light fawn to dark

CHAPTER 2   Primitive Dogs and Pariah Dogs

Indian Pariah Dog

red-brown indicate breeding with imported dogs. Their coat is typically double with a coarse upper coat and soft undercoat.

Author and dog enthusiast M. Krishnan wrote, "[The INDog] is tractable, clever, even sagacious, self-reliant and absolutely incorruptible. It has an extremely hardy constitution and costs next to nothing to feed. There is no better house-dog. It is so clever and willing, you can teach it practically anything, it never makes friends with strangers whatever the bait, and will wake and give voice at the slightest suspicion of anything wrong. It does not keep howling all night, nullifying all attempts at sleep, but barks only when there is good reason. It is this quality, rather than the desire and ability to maul, that is wanted in a watch-dog, and the [INDog] has it..." [from Indog.com]

As evidenced by this quotation, INDogs tend to be both very social and very territorial. They take a light touch when training and get bored easily.

"It should be remembered...that he owes little or nothing to a cruelly indifferent humanity, and that he preserves, as we shall presently see, an innate friendliness which no neglect can quite eradicate."

J.L. Kipling
Beast and Man in India

Photo Courtesy of Daenna Van Mulligen

Xoloitzcuintli

If you've watched Disney Pixar's Coco, you've seen a Xoloitzcuintli (Show-low-eats-QUEENT-lee) in action in the form of Dante, the street dog. Xolos (Show-lows) are primitive dogs indigenous to Mexico. Their history is ancient, and they were once considered guides to the Aztec underworld. Not only are Xolo remains found in ancient burial sites, but the "Colima dog" statues found in burial excavations are evidence of the Xolos' role. Having guided their owners to the underworld, Xolos then battle fierce crocodilian river monsters on their dead owners' behalf.

CHAPTER 2   Primitive Dogs and Pariah Dogs

Also known as Mexican Hairless Dogs, Xolos were once prized as healers and occasionally as a ritual-based sacred meat for priests or nobility. The Aztecs used these dogs as living "hot water bottles," and breeders today claim they are very alert to sickness and aches in their people.

[My Xolo is] my best friend, and he's helped heal parts of me that were broken and made me a better person. These days he teaches college with me (he will be walking in graduation with me on my latest graduate degree) and helps my students with anxiety.

Ryan Wenzel

The Xolo's very name gives an insight into the dogs' personality and place in religious beliefs. It means "he who snatches his food with teeth sharp as obsidian and who is the representative of the god Xolotl." Xolos were so important to the Aztecs, Mayans, and Mexicas that the Spanish conquistadors hunted and killed the dogs to hasten the native populations' conversion to Catholicism. The indigenous people turned loose their Xolos to save them from extinction.

Based on archaeological evidence, Xolos accompanied migrants across the Bering Land Bridge more than 12,000 years ago. Roughly 3,500 years

Photo Courtesy of Breanna Folk

ago, the hairless or mostly hairless condition and lack of premolar teeth resulted from a genetic mutation. The lack of premolars makes it relatively easy to identify archaeological remains with confidence.

The earliest known written evidence for Xolos is reputed to be from Spanish conquistador Fernando Hernandez in the 1500s. He wrote, "A dog of medium size, rather heavily built, and long-bodied in proportion to its height; ears large and erect; tail thick, drooping or carried nearly straight behind; hair nearly absent except for a few coarse vibrissae and generally a sparse coating on the tail, particularly near the tip sometimes a tuft on the crown."

The Xolo is closely related to Peruvian Incan Orchid dogs. Both have long prehensile toes and webbed feet. One of the first US breeders of Xolos, N. Pelham Wright, wrote about his Xolo "...Notes[on my Xolo] touched on her attitude toward other animals, and to fire; her dignity, charm and gaiety; her complete [in]dependence, combined with utter disregard of her owners' wishes; her cleanliness and intense domesticity, as opposed to a sort of inherent vagrancy which resulted ultimately in her disappearance (we never found her again); her insatiable appetite and her cunning in stealing food, as though she were balancing the account of generations of undernourished forebears."

Xolos were officially recognized as Mexican Hairless Dogs (toy) by the American Kennel Club between 1887 and 1957. After that, they were no longer recognized as a breed because of the low numbers. In 2011, they were added back to the AKC breed list as Xoloitzcuintli and have since become more common and popular. They come in three sizes, 10 to 14 inches and 9 to 18 pounds (Toy); 14 to 18 inches and 13 to 22 pounds (Miniature); and 18 to 23 inches and 20 to 31 pounds (Standard).

Like all primitives, Xolos have erect ears. They are generally hairless, or mostly hairless with a topknot or light, thin coat. Their colors include black, grayish black, slate gray, red, liver, or bronze. They may have a dappled hide. Their dewclaws are lower on their legs than on most other domestic dogs and are used almost as a thumb to hold food or toys.

Xolos require special care, including weekly baths and moisturizer during adolescence to control acne. Miniature Xolos heal extremely quickly. They require at least 30 minutes of exercise a day and do not want to be physically separated from their human. Unlike other hairless dogs, Xolos do not sunburn easily and even will tan. However, Xolos with white markings should have limited sun time or wear UV-shirts. Dog sunscreen is not recommended as it may clog pores and cause skin issues.

CHAPTER 2 Primitive Dogs and Pariah Dogs

Xolos also need warm clothing, snowsuits, and snow booties to thrive in cold climates.

When they are puppies, [they get] pimples... After teen dog years most of this disappears. I have one that has oilier skin, so I have to watch her [for pimples]. Every day I put almond oil on ... them. I bath them every two weeks with an enzyme shampoo. I wash their paws every week since they get infections quickly. I get nails and ears done every two weeks since long nails scratch skin, which leads to problems. Now they are older, they have problem with the sun, so they wear UV T-shirts.

Jenny Young, Xolo owner

Carolina Dog

The Carolina Dog is the only primitive dog found in North America and was first identified in the Carolinas. They are found throughout the Southeast. The dog in Old Yeller was probably a Carolina Dog, rather than Disney's Labrador star. Some refer to Carolina Dogs as American Dingoes, but they are not related to dingoes. In fact, DNA testing places them closer to wolves than domestic dogs.

Photo Courtesy of Cori Ludemann

Photo Courtesy of Cori Ludemann

Artwork from early settlers shows small, erect-eared, curved tail dogs following their Native American owners. These were probably Carolina Dogs. Because they were not European dogs, Carolinas were disdained and ignored as mutts, until they were officially discovered by ecologist Dr. I. Lehr Brisbane in the 1970s.

Dr. Brisbane conducted mitochondrial research on wild Carolinas living on the Savannah River in Georgia and discovered that their DNA was far more ancient than domesticated dog mDNA.

CHAPTER 2   Primitive Dogs and Pariah Dogs

Cy Brown, a Carolina Dog owner, wrote this passage that defines what every Carolina Dog owner has experienced: "I love to take her collar off and let her run through the woods uninhibited. She looks perfect that way. Like she was made for it. Without the jingle of her dog tag, it's even easier to lose her in the forest. Eventually, I'll catch a glimpse of her standing on a rock or log, ears perked up, chest poked, tail in a perfect fishhook curve. There's something majestic and primal about it... When I'm ready to leave, I'll open my car door, say her name, and she will pop out of the woods, almost out of nothingness, and into the passenger seat."

My Carolina Dog wore an orange safety vest when hiking in Wyoming because she looked like a small orange coyote or a very large fox. She moved and hunted like a fox and thus was in constant danger of being shot.

Carolinas are fairly small, seventeen to twenty-four inches and thirty-three to seventy pounds. They range from light yellow to deep ginger and have a dense double coat, curved tail and erect, expressive ears. Recently, solid black Carolina Dogs from wild packs have been discovered, although they are not common. Most tan-colored Carolinas have pale shoulder bars and a scent mark about halfway down the tail. They are social and friendly but need constant socialization. Many Carolinas are listed at shelters as shepherd, Lab, and/or chow mixes. It is not until you get them home that you realize that you have a very special dog on your hands.

Identified Breeds of Primitive Dogs

The following dog breeds are included in most lists as primitives or aboriginals. While many of these may not be particularly available as pets, they are still worth knowing about. All primitive dogs have a long history of living with people on practically every continent and this list shows the diversity.

Pariah/dingo group

AfriCanis (Sub-sahara)

Aso (Philippines)

Bali Dog (Bali/Polynesia)

Basenji/Congo Basin Native Dog (Africa)

Canaan Dog (Israel)

Carolina Dog (USA)

Jindo Gae (Korea)

Dingo (Australia)

Khoi/Hottentot Dog (South Africa Cape Area)

Perro Sin Pelo (Peru)

INDog/ (India)

Phu Quoc (Vietnam)

Santhal Hound (India)

Sica (South Africa Natal)

Singing Dog (New Guinea)

Telomian (Malaysia)

Xoloitzcuintli (Mexico)

Greek Greyhound (Greece)

I-Twina (South/East Africa)

Sloughi (Arabia)

Saluki (Iran)

Nordic Spitz Group

Ainu (Hokkaido, Japan)

Finnish Lapphund

Finnish Spitz (Finland)

Iceland Dog (Iceland)

Inuit Dog (Canada)

Karelian Bear Dog (Finland)

Kai (Japan)

Kishu (Honshu, Japan)

Norwegian Lundehund

Norwegian Buhund

Shiba Inu (Honshu, Japan)

Shikoku (Honshu, Japan)

Laikas and Northern

East-Siberian Laika

West-Siberian Laika

Russian-European Laika

Karelian-Finnish Laika

Chukotka sled dog

Kamchatka sled dog

Amur Laika (river Amur)

Reindeer Laika (north Ural)

Yakutian Laika (Yakutia)

Samoyed

Siberian Husky

Prick-Eared Hounds

Cirneco Dell Etna (Sicily)

Ibizan (Majorca)

Kelb-tal-fenek (pharaoh hound) (Malta)

Podenco Portugueso

Podenco Andaluz – (Spain)

Borzoi

Tazi (Western Asia)

Taygan

Russian Gazehound

Shepherds

Azian shepherd

Kavkaz shepherd

Gazehounds

Afghan (Afghanistan)

Azawakh (North Africa)

Chart Polski (Poland)

CHAPTER 2 Primitive Dogs and Pariah Dogs

The Short Version

- We discussed three of the fifty-five primitive dogs; the INDog, Xolo, and Carolina Dog.
- Primitive dogs come from ancient lineages and have always been linked to specific regions.
- Primitives are divided into two types, the Spitz-type and the Primitive-type.
- Primitives are commonly described as independent, suspicious, clever, aloof, sensitive, alert, and stubborn.

CHAPTER 3
Is a Wild Canine or Wild Canine Cross Right for You?

Those who wish to pet and baby wild animals "love" them. But those who respect their natures and wish to let them live normal lives, love them more.

Edwin Way Teale, naturalist

Wild Canine Issues

Ownership of wolves, coyotes, and dingoes and all crosses is determined by state/province and local authorities. Owning pure wolves, coyotes, and dingoes as pets is not advisable. In fact, for 99.9% of people reading this book, even homing a cross is a supremely bad idea. If you are considering a pure wild canine, these issues are even more pronounced.

As you will read, these animals take a lot of work and special handling. If you are willing to live according to your wild canine's attitudes, you may be successful. Otherwise, getting a more domesticable dog breed will be far more successful.

Photo Courtesy of Michelle Proulx W.O.L.F. Sanctuary, Colorado

CHAPTER 3   Is a Wild Canine or Wild Canine Cross Right for You?

Photo Courtesy of Joseph Rembish

Concerns to Consider Before You Bring Home a Cross

Most dog breeds have been deliberately bred over hundreds of years to be social, eager to please, and friendly. Wolves have not and the more wolf genes your cross has, the less social, eager to please, and friendly it will be. The same is even more true for coyotes and dingoes. Because coyotes are not very popular as pets, there have not been attempts to breed docility into them. The purer the coydog or DingoX, the wilder it will be.

Wolf dogs are betwixt and between. They are neither dog nor wolf."

Susan Weidel,
W.O.L.F. Rescue

The unfortunate reality of owning a cross is that it will probably
1. end up chained or otherwise confined
2. be released into the wild where it will die a miserable death
3. be surrendered to a shelter where it will be euthanized
4. be surrendered to an already crowded refuge populated with other crosses whose owners could not handle them.

Yes, there are success stories. Most involve experienced dog owners who have carefully considered and chosen to live with their wild canines. Successful owners understand that these are not trophy pets or status symbols. They understand and accommodate the behaviors that make these animals unique.

Very few success stories involve first-time dog owners or people who acquire a wild canine without considering what they are bringing home. If you are not an experienced dog owner willing to live your life around your wild canine, please stick with more tractable breeds. They will still be a challenge, but not as much as one of these dogs.

"You don't own a wolf dog. The wolf dog owns you. Your entire life will revolve around your wolf dog, if you are a good wolf dog owner. Your wolf dog will want to be with you all the time. You don't leave them at a kennel, and you can't have a stranger come in to take care of them."

former Wyoming wolf dog owners

General Wild Dog Attitudes

While generalizations ignore the outliers, they are still based on truths. The following are the eight generalizations that describe 99% of the wolves, coyotes, dingoes, and their crosses at the heart of this book.

Truth 1: They are highly social and live in a tightly bonded pack, or temporary pack for coyotes.

Truth 2: Their pack structure is defined.

Truth 3: They will challenge lower-status individuals for status.

Truth 4: They are highly territorial.

Truth 5: They have a high prey drive.

Truth 6: They are extremely alert.

Truth 7: They are wary of humans because they want to avoid confrontation.

Truth 8: They begin to respond to outside influences at about age two and become "unpredictable."

If you understand these truths, you are one step closer to understanding crosses.

CHAPTER 3   Is a Wild Canine or Wild Canine Cross Right for You?

The greater the content of wild genes your dog has, the greater the odds that your cross will act like their wild parent. In other words, a 7/8 wolf dog will be far wilder in behavior than a 1/8 wolf dog.

"Wolves should be wolves and dogs should be dogs."

Darlene Kobobel
Colorado Wolf and Wildlife Center

Truth 1: They Are Highly Social and Live in a Tightly Bonded Pack

Wolves, dingoes, and their crosses need other pack members to be happy. They become very stressed if their pack members (human or animal) are absent. Conversely, coyote crosses prefer to be only pets, and they bond very closely to one person. All wild canines will take inexplicable dislikes to certain people, and one of those people might just be a family member.

It is very difficult to leave your wild canine or cross at a kennel because of the liability and vaccination issues (discussed later). They are also very difficult to rehome. Most will be euthanized in a regular shelter because rescues are full.

If you have one of these animals and release it into the wild, it lacks the skills to survive. The individual has no pack, no territory, and no hunting skills. The released wild canine will most probably die of starvation. In addition, release is illegal in many states.

Truths 2 and 3: Their Pack Structure Is Defined and They May Challenge for Status

Photo Courtesy of Terri Martin

Wolves/dingoes/coyotes live in a very defined society and are very status conscious. Within a healthy, established pack, there is always a pack order, and it cannot be violated without the wild canine attempting to reestablish the pecking order.

As your wolf, dingo, or coyote reaches sexual maturity, your wild canine will experiment with dominance. You or other non-alpha pack members can expect to be challenged at this age. These animals also expect that others will respect their status or be punished for challenging them.

Darlene Kobobel, CEO and Director of Colorado Wolf and Wildlife Center, explained that challenging often comes in the form of baring teeth, or in the case of coyotes, biting. If you back down from the challenge, you lose status. However, humans are not physically able to challenge back and win. As Sue Weidel of W.O.L.F. Rescue put it, "If you tussle with a wolf, you will lose."

We had several bites from our wolf dogs. One occurred when our daughter went through the door before the wolf dog. She nipped our daughter in punishment for taking the wolf dog's place in the pack structure. Another time, I tried to take away a bird from our female. She was very unhappy and let me know.

former Wyoming wolf dog owners

CHAPTER 3   Is a Wild Canine or Wild Canine Cross Right for You?

Truth 4: They Are Highly Territorial

A wild canine will defend its home. Crosses also tend to be territorial. It is hard to bring in another animal or person. It may be very difficult to travel with a cross.

When we took them hiking, they were fine with other dogs and people, but the instant we returned home, they became aggressive toward those dogs and people. –former Wyoming wolf dog owners

Truth 5: They Have A High Prey Drive

Wild canines are predators and crosses are no different. The odds are high that a cross will see cats, dogs, livestock of all sizes, wild animals, birds, and children as viable prey. Even a domestic dog that has accepted a child as a pack member can have a lapse of control and attack a screaming

Photo Courtesy of Tracy Hawkins

or running youngster. A child is just too close to a prey species to be safe around wild canines.

Wolves and coyotes in captivity are fascinated by small squeaking children running up and down in front of their enclosures because they sound like injured prey animals.

We were very careful to keep our animals separate. We cared for our son's dog for a few months and had to keep the dog in the basement away from the wolf dogs.

former Wyoming wolf dog owners

Truth 6: They Are Extremely Alert

Wolves, dingoes, or coyotes and their crosses are very alert to their surroundings. They will investigate every sound, movement, scent, and change in your house. Coydogs tend not to do as well with changes as wolf dogs. Crosses also like their surroundings to remain the same.

Truth 7: They Are Wary of Humans

Your dog may lose its wariness depending on how young your cross begins socialization, the type and amount of dog genes, and your cross's personality. However, it will generally always have a hard time with new people.

The higher the wild canine gene content the more skittish your cross will be. It may also be extremely particular about who they accept. At W.O.L.F., certain wolves have decided they do not like some staff and volunteers. For their safety, these people are not allowed around the specific wolves. Captive coyotes have the same issue.

> **HELPFUL TIP**
> **Think Carefully**
>
> Wild canines and crosses can be extremely difficult to manage, and little research has been done on things like how they respond to vaccines or anesthesia. Some vets, groomers, and boarding facilities may refuse service to you and your dog. Make sure you're aware of the limitations you may face having a wild canine or cross as a pet.

Truth 8: They Become "Unpredictable"

Wolf dogs and coydogs have a reputation of being extremely unpredictable. Successful owners state that this is not necessarily true. What is true is that your cross will begin to respond differently to outside stimuli as it reaches sexual maturity. Many of the experts I consulted agreed that by two years of age, your wolf, coyote, or dingo cross will begin to show more and more wild traits. They will also begin to express their dominance. If you are a knowledgeable and dedicated owner, these wild traits can be assimilated into the home. If you are not, these behaviors will cause issues.

"Wolf dogs are not like dogs. They aren't yes-men."

Susan Weidel,
W.O.L.F. Rescue

Housing

You will need a very tall fence or covered enclosure for a wolf, coyote, or dingo or their crosses. Wolves can scale twelve-foot fences without hesitation. Your six-foot privacy fence will NOT keep in a cross determined to roam.

States where wolf or wolf cross ownership is legal may have specific enclosure designs for them, so check your state laws. The Gray Wolf Conservation organization recommends the following outdoor containment system for wolves and wolf crosses.

- Space from neighbors
    - Howling is very natural and very annoying for neighbors
    - High noise or traffic areas are very stressful
- Land area
    - 1 acre of enclosed space for one animal. This is the bare minimum for two
    - Add at least ½ an acre per additional animal
    - Drainage adequate to provide dry areas when wet
    - Sturdy chew-resistant shelters
    - Vegetation that is NOT near the fence or that may fall near the fence as the animal can use it to climb out
- Primary fence enclosure
    - Total height must be eight feet: six feet of chain link with a two-foot angled extension (in hang)
    - Electric wire is recommended at the top of the fence
    - All primary fences and gates should be 9-gauge wire with two-inch squares
    - Concrete wall with reinforced mesh extending two feet into ground and attached to the base of the chain link fence
    - Four feet of chain link lying flat on the ground in the enclosure. May be covered with dirt, rocks, etc.
- Perimeter fence enclosure
    - The perimeter fence be at least five feet tall, and five feet away from the primary fence
- Gates
    - Entrances must have a double gate to prevent escapes and be six feet tall, built within the taller fence, with secure, lockable latches
    - Gate framework must be on the exterior to prevent climbing

CHAPTER 3   Is a Wild Canine or Wild Canine Cross Right for You?

With our first wolf dog, we tied him on a cable system. At some point, he broke the ¼" cable and went exploring. He was hit and killed by a train. Wolf dogs will stand in the middle of a road or train track and stare at you. They won't move.

former Wyoming wolf dog owners

Dingoes need equally elaborate housing arrangements. The government of the North West Territory in Australia describes a necessary confinement system for pure dingoes. This is probably also appropriate for crosses.

- A minimum area of approximately 220 square meters (2,370 square feet)
- A chain mesh fence using 3.15mm wire (0.12") with a maximum mesh spacing of 50mm (two inches).
- This fence should extend into the ground at least thirty centimeters (one foot).
- A two-meter (seventy-eight inches) high fence with an additional 0.5-meter (19 inch) in hang
- A one meter (thirty-nine inches) pinned mesh footing from the base of the fence into the enclosure to stop digging out
- Enrichment items within the enclosure such as large logs and rocks
- A weatherproof sleeping area

The Wisconsin Department of Natural Resources has minimum requirements for captive coyotes.

- Cover top pens
    - A covered top pen must provide a minimum of 144 square feet for up to two animals
    - For each additional animal, add fifty square feet
    - Covered top pen height must be six feet
- Open top pens
    - Open top pens must have a minimum of 1,000 square feet
    - Open top pens must have eight-foot walls with three feet of inward slanted fencing

They need places to hide and den. Coyotes also like to dig, so having a set-up similar to dingoes and wolves with dig-proof chain-link fencing would be a good idea.

Exercise

Wolves travel up to thirty miles per day; coyotes at least ten miles; and dingoes about twenty-five miles a day. A cross requires massive amounts of exercise to keep it from becoming destructive. Walking these animals on a leash is probably not going to be very successful. First, they are extremely powerful. Second, they are very wary of people and will try to avoid them. Third, rabies vaccines are not recognized for use on wolves, coyotes, or their crosses. If your wild canine bites a person or another dog, you may be legally required to euthanize your wild canine immediately.

"Displaced energy from boredom or lack of exercise equals destructive and aggressive behaviors."

Susan Weidel,
W.O.L.F. Rescue

Coyote crosses like to explore and may go off for days at a time. A once a day walk is not enough for most coydogs. They need concentrated exercise two or three times a day. Kenneling a coyote/coydog is a fast way to end up with a neurotic animal.

Training

Wolves do not respond well to physical punishment. According to Sue Weidel of W.O.L.F. Rescue, physically punishing a wolf cross is likely to result in an attack. You are weaker than a fully-grown wolf and lack the bite force a wolf, especially the force a scared or angry one will generate. If you normally resort to physical punishment to train a dog, avoid getting a wolf dog.

The fastest way to train a wolf dog is to withhold affection. This takes time and patience. According to wolf owners, frowning or ignoring them after bad behavior has the best results.

Coyotes or dingoes may be resistant to training. Crosses may be slightly more tractable, depending on the type and amount of their dog heritage. As with wolves, physical punishment does not work with coyotes or dingoes or their crosses and they are less interested in fitting into your pack than a wolf or wolf cross might be.

CHAPTER 3 Is a Wild Canine or Wild Canine Cross Right for You?

According to various owners, housetraining is generally simple with wolves and wolf crosses and more complex with coyotes or dingoes and their crosses.

Food

For best health, wolf and wolf crosses must be fed meat-based, high-energy dry dog food and five to ten percent of their diet must be whole prey items such as bones, skin, and hair. Wild wolves require about five pounds of food a day. A wolf cross will eat as much food as it can, according to wolf cross owners.

Photo Courtesy of Kylie Settler

Arkansas state law (20-19-404) specifies that a wolf/cross must be fed a meat-based protein content of twenty-five percent and a crude fat content of fifteen percent, unless otherwise advised by a licensed veterinarian. W.O.L.F. warns that wolves are sensitive to fat and a high-fat diet may lead to pancreatitis. High protein feeds are generally top-shelf brands and are correspondingly more expensive, roughly twice the cost compared to least expensive brands.

W.O.L.F. feeds captive wolf dogs with raw meat (chicken, beef, mutton), and once a week they get raw bones. The wolves' favorite tends to be game meat donated by local hunters. All meat must be defatted. Pork results in diarrhea. Very rarely, the wolves get a tiny bit of bacon or hotdogs. They also love raw eggs.

Feeding a wolf cross pup is different than feeding a domesticated puppy. Meat supplementation begins far earlier, and kibble lacks the nutrients the pup needs to grow. Wolf crosses often come to W.O.L.F. with skeletal issues because of an inadequate diet as both pups and adults. They have been surrendered as much as twenty pounds underweight. It is extremely expensive to feed a wolf cross properly.

A properly fed dingo may live twenty or more years while a dingo on a domestic dog diet may only live seven or eight years. Dingoes do best on a whole food diet. That means the fur, feathers, feet, heads, and bones. The Dingo Den Rescue recommends removing guts to lessen the odds of parasites. If feeding a carcass to your dingo is a bit too gruesome, meats like lean beef, lamb, poultry, fish, pig trotters, ears and snouts, and kangaroo is appropriate, especially when supplemented with fresh eggs, pureed leafy greens, wild fruit, and grasses. Dingoes do not process fat particularly well either.

Coyotes are omnivores and need meat, vegetables, and other items. One of the most important food items a coyote or coyote cross needs are bones. This keeps their bite very strong so they can still hunt if they manage to escape captivity. Coyote pups have equally complex diets and puppy kibble, especially soaked in cow's milk, is very bad for them.

Before feeding raw eggs to a cross with domesticated dog genes, you may want to speak to a knowledgeable vet because raw egg whites can be harmful to domestic dogs. Current veterinary information finds that egg whites contain avidin. This biotin (Vitamin B7) inhibitor may cause a B7 deficiency. However, the amount of avidin that causes a biotin deficiency is unknown.

If you are looking for the best possible diet for your wolf or coyote or cross, look at a BARF (Biologically Appropriate Raw Food) diet. This is a complex combination of raw meat and organs, bones, vegetables, and fruits that mimics a natural wild diet.

Medical Care

Providing medical care for your wild canine or cross may be problematic. Your first concern is to find a vet that will accept a wild canine and who knows the specialized treatments a wild canine may require.

Wolf crosses handle pain medication and sedation far differently than domestic dogs. It may take considerably more anesthesia to sedate a wolf dog. Wolf crosses also come out of anesthesia almost immediately and inattentive vets have had wolf crosses stand up and fall off the table as soon as the reversing agent was administered.

Several American vets expressed reservations about treating wild canines because of their pack and territorial behaviors. If you are bringing a wild canine or cross to your vet for the first time, always advise them before you walk in. They may require additional safety measures like muzzles.

The most important issue for wolves, coyotes, and their crosses' health is rabies vaccinations and the legality for inoculating wild canines and the unknown effectiveness on wild canines. At the time of writing, Australia is rabies free and so this does not affect dingoes.

The FDA states that the rabies vaccine is not approved for use on wild canines and their crosses. If it is given to wild canines or crosses, it is considered "off-label" or "extra use." Because of the off-label status regarding the use of rabies vaccine in wild canines, vets may refuse to inoculate both pure and cross canines for legal reasons. In addition, because of the off-label status, many states do not recognize the effectiveness of the rabies vaccine when given to a cross or pure blood canine. If the wild canine or cross bites, it can be euthanized, and the brain sent for rabies testing because of this legal issue.

> **HELPFUL TIP**
> **Vet Care**
>
> Some veterinarians may refuse to treat wild canines and crosses. Medications, vaccinations, and anesthetics work very differently on wild canines. Some, like rabies shots, are not approved for use on wild canines. You may need to find a vet who specializes in exotic animals to treat your wild canine or cross.

Safety

The biting force of a wolf and a dingo is truly astounding. Both can bite down at an amazing 1,500 pounds. In comparison, a Rottweiler has a biting force of 328 pounds, while the apparently most feared dog in America, the pit bull, comes in at a measly 238 pounds. Coyote bite force probably ranks about the same as a pit bull. Most coyote bite force statements compare them to "a medium-sized dog."

A wolf or dingo can crush long bones like femurs in two or three bites. Their jaws are incredibly powerful. If you put your wild canine or cross in a situation where it is scared or angry, a human or other animal will stand a high risk of severe injury or even death.

While I was in the process of researching this book, one of my friends sent a text about her mother's recent experience with a husky-wolf cross. Paraphrased, this was her story.

"My elderly mom and her cousin were visiting a family member with a 7-year-old husky-wolf cross. The dog is very territorial and easily threatened, and the owners were trying to introduce the dog to the visitors. The women sat down, put their hands under their legs as instructed, and the dog was allowed to approach them, on leash and muzzled. The wolf dog immediately lunged at my mom. She ended up with only a black eye, but the wolf dog went for her face."

Homeowner's Insurance

Before you bring home a wild canine or cross, check with your insurance company. If you do not do this and then notify your insurance company about your new pet or change companies, you may lose or be denied insurance.

My personal homeowner's insurance company explained that they required a customer to present the wolf dog or coydog for a "meet and greet." If the animal failed this test, you would be declined coverage. Other insurance companies may have far different rules.

Some states require you to carry liability insurance if you own a wolf or wolf cross. This requirement is spelled out in state statutes. Your homeowner's insurance may require you to carry liability insurance or have a special rider included on your policy.

Always check BEFORE bringing home an animal. Finding out after your wild canine bites someone that your insurance does not cover those damages can be extremely expensive.

Volkosobs

An interesting anecdote that incorporates all the aspects of safety, wolf dog breeding, and how wolf dogs act is the tale of the Volkosobs and how they were developed.

The Russian border patrol uses trained wolf dogs called Volkosobs instead of domesticated dogs. These crosses (25% wolf, 75% dog) are far more focused than domesticated dogs and find drugs, bombs, and criminals in less than twenty seconds, compared to four minutes for a dog. Handlers say domestic dogs need to play for a few minutes and look around while the Volkosobs are all business. They are also far more aggressive than trained K-9s and rarely bother with arms or legs, preferring to go for the throat.

However, Volkosobs are not random dog-wolf crosses. All Volkosobs are descended from one wolf bitch, Naida, who was, by all accounts, unique. Naida sought out male dogs to breed with and was far more sociable with humans than typical wolves.

In attempting to develop Volkosobs, more than two hundred wolf dog puppies from random crossings were deemed undesirable because they were unable to overcome their distrust of strange humans. With this in mind, the odds that a random wolf and dog crossing will result in a social animal are remote.

The Short Version

- You do not own a wolf dog (or coyote or dingo). It owns you.
- Wolves and dingoes are highly social and live in a tightly bonded pack.
- Wolves and dingoes have a defined pack structure.
- Wild canines will challenge for status.
- Wild canines are highly territorial.
- Wild canines have a high prey drive.
- Wild canines are extremely alert.
- Wild canines are wary of humans because they want to avoid confrontation.
- Wild canines begin to respond to outside influences at about age two and become "unpredictable."

CHAPTER 4
Is a Primitive Dog Right for You?

You cannot share your life with a dog... or a cat, and not know perfectly well that animals have personalities and minds and feelings.

Jane Goodall, biologist

Photo Courtesy of Steven Berry

Primitive dogs come with their own unique challenges. They may look more dog-like than wolf-like, but they have survived for thousands of years living by their wits just as their wolf ancestors have done. Primitive dogs are truly "couch wolves." They choose to live with us because it makes their life easier, not because they have been bred for a life of servitude. All primitive dogs, including those like sled dogs that have been selectively bred for generations, have similar attitudes and behaviors.

The wolf dog you bought may actually fall into the primitive dog category, since very few wolf dogs have much pure wolf DNA. Most come from Spitz-type primitive dogs like Siberian Huskies or Malamutes crossed with German Shepherds. If you've gotten a "wolf" dog or a wannabe dire wolf, this may be the right section for you to read.

"A domestic dog is like dealing with a two-year-old child. A primitive is like dealing with a teenager."

Cori Ludeman,
dog trainer and Carolina Dog owner

CHAPTER 4   Is a Primitive Dog Right for You?

The Dog de Jour (The Dog of the Day)

Movies and TV shows make certain dog breeds popular. Collies, Jack Russell Terriers, German Shepherds, and Dalmatians have all gone through a rise in popularity followed by high numbers showing up in shelters and rescues. The dog on the TV screen has undergone thousands of hours of training and is handled by a very experienced trainer. That clever dog still comes with normal dog urges and problems, like deafness in Dalmatians and hyperactivity in Jack Russells. Before you buy the *dog de jour*, take time to learn about the real dog, not the movie version.

The current *dog de jour* is a primitive breed, the Siberian Husky, and its popularity is high because of *Game of Thrones* dire wolf characters. Siberian Huskies are the epitome of primitive dog. Huskies are destructive, high energy, need constant exercise, are escape artists, and have the reputation of being hard to train. Because their owners did not research the breed before getting one, these dogs are also showing up in shelters in large numbers.

Before you voluntarily bring home a primitive breed, consider the following.

Photo Courtesy of Joleen Smith

What to Consider Before Bringing Home a Primitive Dog

HELPFUL TIP: Primitive Dog Attitudes

Primitive dogs have very similar attitudes. Thinking of them as a teenager or a cat in a dog suit will help you understand your primitive dog's attitude toward life. You are dealing with a smart dog with a sense of humor and a desire to be your partner, not your servant.

Most successful primitive dog owners will tell you that owning one is an amazing, once in a lifetime experience. However, they are not for every person or family.

A primitive dog will be a partner more readily than it will be a servant. These dogs are the epitome of Rudyard Kipling's First Friend from the *Just So Stories*. In *The Cat That Walked by Itself*, Kipling imagines how and why dogs took up with humans. The main reason is because life was a bit more pleasant with humans than out in the wild. Since dogs were the first, according to Kipling's story, they are known forever as the First Friend.

Our First Friend probably moved in with humans as captured puppies or because life with humans was marginally easier. The first dogs acted as garbage eaters, early guards, bedwarmers, and occasionally as a food source. They may have helped with hunts or eventually guarded encampments and herds.

For thousands of years, these were dogs' only jobs – to live on the outskirts of human habitation and help when they felt like it. Servility and specialization were bred in later. Even primitives with extensive selective breeding still maintain the primitive characteristics of their less manipulated cousins. Sled dogs, like Inuit dogs or Malamutes, will always be primitive even though they have been selectively bred for endurance and strength.

This primitive-human relationship was based on mutual self-interest. The primitive dog still operates on the theory that it will do what it likes on its terms, not yours. The eventual desire to serve as retrievers, herding dogs, flea traps, rat catchers, or fighting dogs was bred into dogs over hundreds of years by humans. Thus, the rules for dealing with primitive dogs are very different from the average domestic dog.

CHAPTER 4   Is a Primitive Dog Right for You?

Photo Courtesy of Breanna Folk

General Attitudes

As we've said, primitive dogs are very different from domesticated dogs. The ones that come from wild or feral stock tend to have very "wolf-like" wild characteristics even down to biology like once a year estrus cycle, commonly known as "going into heat." Of course, within every generalization, there are exceptions. If your primitive is very domesticated, you have lucked out!

Of all the identified primitive dog breeds, all are generally independent, suspicious, clever, unpredictable, aloof, sensitive, alert, and stubborn. Once they bond to their family, they are not easily rehomed.

These are all generally negative stereotypes. If you buy into these, you will have more of an issue living with your primitive. Let's rename them as tenacious, engaged, determined, empathetic, and honest. They bond closely with family and will stick with you because they want to. Think about these dogs as "cats in dog suits," and you will have a pretty good idea of what you are dealing with.

[INDogs] are street smart [and] very intelligent.... If trained well, they make the best guard dogs, too. Most of them are polite [dogs].

INDog owner

The three primitives discussed in this book all show those general characteristics.

Independent and Aloof (Tenacious)

Primitive dog owners liken their living arrangements with primitive dogs as being more like roommates, rather than dog and master. Very commonly, trainers may think that these dogs are untrainable. That is very untrue – these dogs are quite trainable... on their terms. If your primitive sees the point, it will practically train itself. As long as you are smarter than your primitive, you can outthink it. Otherwise, you are in for a wild ride.

[INDogs] are the smartest, hardiest, and [lowest] maintenance pets you could get.

INDog owner

CHAPTER 4 Is a Primitive Dog Right for You?

Your primitive will be glad to see you, and may be very good with other people, but think of them as giant cats. When they want attention, they will lavish it on you. When they do not, they walk away. Your primitive is in it for him, not for you. According to Xolo owner, Sydney Brooke Cooper, Xolos are Velcro dogs. They pick out one person in the family and that is their person and the Xolo wants to be with this person at all times.

My Xolo is a bit suspicious [about strangers], but mostly they step away – no biting or aggression.

Alisia OroBello, Xolo owner

Suspicious and Alert (Engaged)

Primitive dogs are highly aware of their surroundings, like their wild ancestor, the wolf. Anything that is new must be investigated. My Carolina Dog spent hours sitting on a picnic table on a raised porch, watching everything that went on in the neighborhood. She was the nosy old lady peeking out through the curtains. In her fourteen years, she growled at three people. Two were our next-door neighbors who eventually set fire to our garage. We knew they were creepy. She knew they were threats.

> **HELPFUL TIP**
> **The Dog De Jour**
>
> Before you buy or adopt a dog made popular in movies or TV, take the time to find out what you are adopting. The movie star dog is well trainer and professionally handled. Your dog will not be professionally trained or handled and will not act like the movie star dog.

Xolo owner Jenny Young said that the best and worst trait about Xolos is the barking. They are so alert they hear and know everything that is going on outside the house and let their people know. Sydney Brooke Cooper describes Xolo aloofness as suspicion. INDog owners value their dogs for their alertness and territoriality.

[One time] we had some friends come over late one night, and ... parked their big van in the driveway. The next morning when we let Sherlock [a Carolina Dog] out, he immediately started barking and growling with hackles raised at the van. This was something novel in his environment, and he was on high alert right away. The same thing happened one day after we moved a potted plant to a different portion of the yard.

Nicole Strauss, Carolina Dog owner

Photo Courtesy of Owen Wood

Clever and Stubborn (Determined)

Primitives tend to become bored easily and do not enjoy concentrated training. You might get one or two repetitions and then find it is time to move on. My Carolina Dog loved agility courses. Once. More than once through all the obstacles and she would trot off and refuse to cooperate. The training had to be fun and quick. You will find this trait in all primitive breeds.

My oldest Xolo opens doors so we had to switch handles on bedroom doors (no levers – only knobs). The middle boy gets ice out of the automatic ice on the fridge.

Lisa Rhoades Jett, Xolo owner

One Search and Rescue professional rescued a Carolina Dog and thought he would make a great search dog. Turns out he will go all day with her shepherd search dog but has no interest in following a scent trail.

(My Carolina Dog) will pick out a piece of mulch or wood...really taking his time getting the perfect piece. He then holds it between his upper and lower incisors and uses the mulch to comb the inside of his leg hair.

Nicole Strauss, Carolina Dog owner

Sensitive (Empathetic and Honest)

Your primitive may have an almost uncanny ability to spot sick, injured, or emotionally upset family members. Xolos were bred to comfort sick people and their owners describe how sensitive they are to changes. One trainer taught her Shibu to act as her hands. Once the dog figured it out, he self-taught what she needed.

The unconditional love and fierce loyalty you receive in return for a few scraps of food doesn't remain confined to your home, or to your farm...I am a better person [for owning an INDog] –INDog owner

My Carolina Dog certified as a therapy dog, and she loved to go into nursing homes. She would dance and smile when she approached someone but then immediately settled into a leaning sit for as long as the person wanted to pet her. When she sensed they were tired, she'd give a quick nose to hand and move to the next person.

If you think that corporal punishment is appropriate for a dog, a primitive is not for you. They are more cat-like than dog-like and do not respond well to discipline.

When we are home, they bark, but when we welcome strangers in, they stop being badass and become cuddly bears. –INDog owner

Denning Behavior

Most primitives like to den. Carolina Dogs are notorious for digging snout pits – holes large and deep enough to stick their snouts in. Your yard will be full of little snout holes and big dens.

Spitz-types love cold weather and will make snow dens. Because primitives like to den, they are generally very easy to crate train and appreciate a cave of their own in the house.

My Xolo always has to dig in his bed. Always has to be under all blankets, never on top. Also, they have long webbed nails that are almost prehensile meaning it's as if they can grab things!

Sydney Brooke Cooper, Xolo owner

Prey Drive

Primitives have an extremely high prey drive. Anything small and moving is fair game. Early socialization may let you have another animal around or keep wildlife safe, but there is no guarantee. My Carolina Dog took birds out of the air, was a far better mouser than any cat, and killed her share of prairie dogs and marmots. She was raised with cats and inside cats were safe. Outside cats were fair game. She would chase livestock or wild game, but she would also obey commands to leave them alone. She would actively defend camp sites from marauding cows and squirrels, chasing them to the edge of her camp territory.

CHAPTER 4   Is a Primitive Dog Right for You?

Prey drive!? (My Carolina Dog has caught) two deer, one turkey, two chickens, [and] two squirrels. Best loving smart dog I have ever been around.

Michael Hall, Carolina Dog owner

When it comes to children, every dog is an individual. My Carolina Dog adored babies and tolerated toddlers as long as she had an escape route. However, as with all dogs, small children should always be supervised. A running, squeaking child is just too tempting.

(Our INDog) can't stand human babies around my parents. He often hunts small creatures and gifts them to us. Seeing small dead animals every morning is little uneasy.

INDog owner

Housing

Primitives can either be very hard or very easy to house train. Some people report that they are cat-like in their ability to show them once and they are housetrained forever; other people have far more trouble. The secret to house training primitive dogs seems to be consistency and patience.

My Carolina housetrained herself in a matter of days.

Cory Ludeman, dog trainer and Carolina Dog owner

You may also need a yard with improved fencing. These are diggers and climbers. Yours may not want to escape or they may be constantly going walk-about.

Exercise

If you like to run or walk, you will probably enjoy a primitive, because you will be doing a lot of both. If you prefer a sedentary life, these are not the dogs for you. A bored primitive is a destructive primitive. All primitives love to run, but Spitz-types truly need to run. They are bred to endure cold weather marathons while pulling sleds. A short walk will not make much of a dent in their energy level.

My Carolina Dog liked nothing better than a three-hour hike. At rest points, she would sit beside you and lean on you, the highest compliment she could give.

Most of these dogs do need activities to keep them physically busy and that in return, keeps them emotionally busy as well. They're so smart. If they get bored, they can become destructive.

Sydney Brooke Cooper, Xolo owner

Food

Feeding a primitive is relatively easy. Choose quality dog food and feed appropriate amounts. It is possible for a primitive to become overweight, but it is less likely than with a more domesticated dog.

When choosing food, read the label, not the advertising. The first three ingredients should be meat (including fish) but never meat meal, bone meal, by-products, or digests. These four ingredients are what is scraped off the slaughterhouse floor or from diseased, not-fit-for-human consumption livestock. Avoid corn, soy, and wheat in all forms. Dyes are also not good for humans or pets, so make sure there are not dyes whose only purpose is to make the food look more appealing to you.

With the right diet, these dogs do not smell at all, unlike pedigreed ones that have a distinct dog smell.

INDog owner

Training the Primitive

Primitives have a reputation for being stubborn and untrainable. In reality, it is very possible to train a primitive. According to Couch Wolves, a website dedicated to primitive dogs, there are three requirements for successful training. The first is currency. Your primitive will work for pay.

Next, you must have teamwork. Your primitive has worked with humans for thousands of years. It comes from a long line of cooperative behaviors within the pack. Your primitive will work with you but never for you.

Finally, you need patience. You will need it for both you and your dog. Your primitive will do what you want it to, provided it sees the point of the exercise. Having a sense of humor will help a lot. Your primitive has a sense of humor. Enjoy it.

"You really have to be thinking [with Xolos] all the time. They open doors, they open crates. This is a primitive dog. They're extremely intelligent." –Kay Lawson in "This Hairless Mexican Dog Has a Storied, Ancient Past"

The Short Version

- Primitive dogs choose to live with us because it makes their life easier, not because they have been bred for a life of servitude.
- This primitive-human relationship was based on mutual self-interest. The primitive dog still operates on the theory that it will do what it likes on its terms, not yours.
- Primitives have an extremely high prey drive.
- Primitives have a reputation for being stubborn and untrainable. They are extremely trainable, on their own terms.

CHAPTER 5
Acquiring Your Dog

When looking to adopt a new dog, the most important thing to consider is always the energy of the dog and how the dog will fit in with your lifestyle and your family.

Cesar Millan, dog trainer

Adopting versus Buying

The two main ways to acquire a dog are either through adopting or buying from a breeder. Each one has benefits and drawbacks. If you are buying a wolf cross, be aware that at least 80% of wolf dogs will not see their third birthday because of the issues we are discussing.

Adopting from a shelter or rescue means you may be saving a life. In the United States alone, 2.7 million cats and dogs a year are euthanized. Many are sent to shelters or rescues because their family got the wrong animal for their household and either cannot or will not keep them. This is particularly true with wolf crosses.

Buying can involve you in the ugly world of puppy mills, even for primitive dogs and wolf crosses. As these have become more popular, they have unfortunately become a source for money for disreputable breeders.

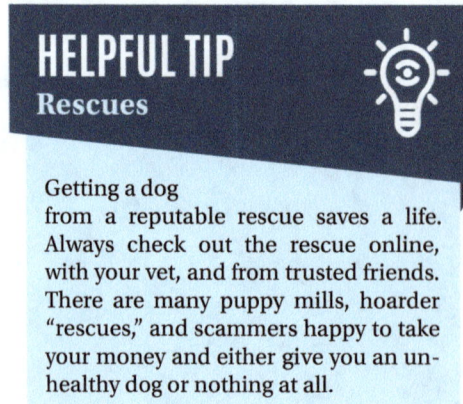

HELPFUL TIP
Rescues

Getting a dog from a reputable rescue saves a life. Always check out the rescue online, with your vet, and from trusted friends. There are many puppy mills, hoarder "rescues," and scammers happy to take your money and either give you an unhealthy dog or nothing at all.

According to W.O.L.F., that expensive wolf dog puppy probably is not a wolf dog at all. It is probably a husky, malamute, or similar dog. In fact, backyard breeders commonly cross Malamutes and German Shepherds. White pups are labeled Arctic wolves, gray ones are timber wolves, and big ones are buffalo wolves. There may be wolf in there somewhere but not enough to justify the outrageous price. They may also be badly inbred and unhealthy.

CHAPTER 5 Acquiring Your Dog

Finding a Reputable Rescue

Finding a reputable rescue or shelter is important. As you begin your search, start with trusted resources. Veterinarians will have a pretty good idea about what shelters or rescues are reputable. They may not come right out and tell you that the shelter is not good, so listen to what they are not saying, in addition to their probable lack of enthusiasm about the shelter.

If there are reviews online, look at those. While most people prefer to gripe rather than praise, you should still read the reviews carefully. A litany of sick dog tales is a warning sign. You may be able to get references from the shelter or rescue as well.

In the United States, reputable rescues and most non-governmentally run shelters will be a registered 501(c)(3) charity.

You should be able to find this documentation online, either on the shelter website or through the IRS website. Some governmental shelters will have an associated 501(c)(3) organization to help handle monetary donations.

Check on the board of directors and see if there are volunteers associated with the rescue. There are hoarders who run "rescues," and these less-than-reputable sources will have no board of directors and no volunteers.

Does the rescue run regular adoption events? If they do, they are generally legitimate. This will not apply to wild canine rescues because the adoption requirements are far more stringent than for domestic dog rescues.

Next, visit the rescue. If they do not allow visitors, do not patronize the establishment. The rescue or shelter should be clean and the animals well fed and clean. Backyard breeders and puppy mills are often dirty, or the animals are not well socialized. Kennels and enclosures should be proper sizes for their occupants.

Watch how the dogs act around the staff. Are they glad to see the staff or frightened by them? Does the staff enjoy interacting with the dogs? Do animals have toys or other means of mental stimulation? How much does the staff know about each dog? Is the dog tested for triggers like food aggression, dog aggression, and child tolerance? This is especially important if you have children or other pets at home. Ask where their animals come from. Puppy mills who portray themselves as rescues tend to breed their own "rescues" for resulting pups.

Expect to be interviewed by a good rescue. You may be asked why you want a specific breed and who will care for the dog daily. They may ask for proof that you can have a dog, especially if you rent rather than own your own home. They may ask who your veterinarian will be. They want to know if their dog is going to a good home. To that end, they should ask you to sign a contract regarding your new dog's care and allow you to return the dog within a certain amount of time.

A backyard breeder or puppy mill just wants to make money and probably will not offer any contract or guarantees. A reputable breeder or rescue will not allow you to take home a pup under six weeks of age. Current trainer and veterinary advice suggest that six to twelve weeks of age corresponds to prime socialization period (for domestic dogs) and introducing a puppy at this age helps to build resiliency. A pup under six weeks of age is still learning dog manners from the mother and removing it early can have lifelong consequences including nipping and aggression.

A good shelter or rescue will have a vet either on staff or on call. You can contact the vet and ask about the dog. They should have immunization and health records that you can examine and have sent to your own veterinarian.

> **HELPFUL TIP**
> **Wild Canine Rescues**
>
> Wild canine rescues will require substantial effort. Not all rescues adopt out as the rescues know that the odds of a successful placement is low. Adopting a wild canine is a lifetime commitment and your life will revolve around your wild canine.

CHAPTER 5 Acquiring Your Dog

Wolf Dog and Dingo Specific Rescues

If you are interested in adopting from a wolf dog rescue, you will have to provide proof that you are a qualified and responsible owner. Many of the animals have gone through a great deal of trauma and may not be emotionally or mentally able to change homes yet again after you've adopted them. As such, a legitimate rescue will make certain that you understand that this is a lifetime commitment. Because of irresponsible breeders and buyers, wolf dog sanctuaries are full.

Following are sample adoption requirements from Howling Woods Farm, a wolf dog rescue. You can expect to see equally rigorous adoption requirements from any reputable rescue.

- Completion of on-line adoption application
- Is legal in your state/county/city to have a wild canine?
- Verify presence of a companion canine for your adopted animal and share enclosure
- Spacious, secure containment
- Phone number of vet who cares for current animals
- Home check to verify adequacy of containment
- Completion of adoption contract
- Adoption donation

  Sample Adoption from Dingo Den
- Personal information
- Experience with captive and wild dingoes
- Personal interest in dingoes
- Lifestyle and home
- Detailed plan of yard or enclosure
- Does your home include children, persons with disabilities, other pets?
- Do your neighbors have any of the above?
- Adoption donation

Photo Courtesy of Jason Stockmyer

Importing a Dog

If you have fallen in love with a dog in another country or want to adopt a primitive dog from its home, you will have to import the dog. In the United States, Canada, and Australia, there are stringent rules that govern importing animals.

It is illegal to import a wild animal into the United States, Canada, or Australia without proper permitting from the government and from CITES (the Convention on International Trade in Endangered Species of Wild Fauna and Flora). In addition, wild animal crosses are protected under CITES and require a CITES permit.

Scammers will promise to import a wild animal or even domesticated one for you and end up taking your money.

What follows is a description of importation requirements for pets into the United States. Canada and Australia will have similar requirements. Your new dog will require:

- A health certificate from a licensed vet
- A valid rabies certificate, depending on the country of origin. Check the CDC website for information on which countries are considered at risk
- If your dog is coming from a place with foot and mouth disease or screwworms, you will have additional documentation

USDA APHIS (Animal and Plant Health Inspection Service) Animal Care requires additional paperwork if you plan to adopt out or sell your dog. Since crosses are very pack oriented, bringing in one with the express intent to transfer it to a new home may result in trauma for the cross.

US Customs and Border Protection also may have additional paperwork. Contact the office at your port of entry into the United States to see what you will need. Your state may have additional entry requirements including quarantine. And finally, the airline or shipping company will have regulations of their own.

It is not a simple operation to import an animal. Keep in mind there are literally millions of dogs in the United States, Canada, and Australia that deserve a safe, loving home.

Legally Owning a Wolf Dog, Coydog, or Dingo/DingoX

If you are interested in adopting a wild canine cross, always check your state, provincial, or territorial laws. There is no one blanket law in the United States, Canada, or Australia that covers ownership of crosses or pure-blooded canines.

The appendices include to-date legal requirements on owning wild canines or crosses. This information is as current as of the publication date. Cities and/or counties may have stricter restrictions, over and above state/provincial law. Please check with an animal control officer or your local ordinances to ensure that you are within the law.

Note that primitive dogs are not included in the appendices. For legal purposes, primitives are considered domesticated dogs.

Appendix 1 covers current (2019) United States laws. Appendix 2 deals with 2019 Canada laws. Appendix 3 includes 2019 Australian laws.

Photo Courtesy of Christian Coombe

CHAPTER 5 Acquiring Your Dog

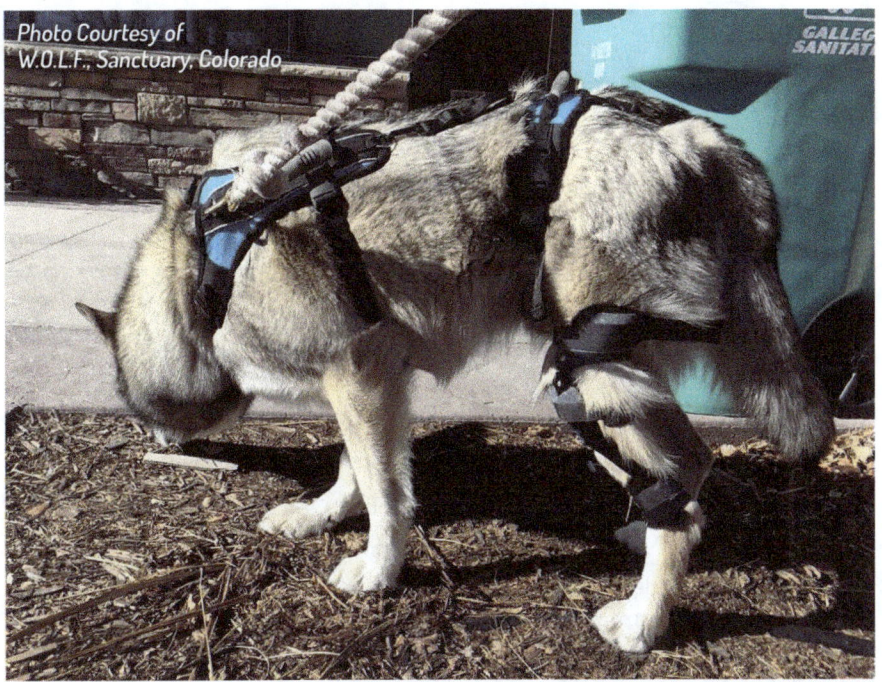

Photo Courtesy of W.O.L.F. Sanctuary, Colorado

The Short Version

- Adopting from a shelter or rescue means you are saving a life.
- If you are interested in adopting from a wild canine rescue, you will have to provide proof that you are a qualified and responsible owner.
- Wild canine shelters are full.
- Importing a dog is not easy.
- Check your state/province/territory, city, and county laws BEFORE acquiring a wild canine.

CHAPTER 6
Preparing Your Home for Your Wild Canine

I had a very famous trainer tell me once, "You can usually train a wild animal but never tame a wild animal, ever." They are always going to be wild, no matter what anybody says.

Jack Hanna, zookeeper

Anytime you introduce a new family member to your home, take the time to make sure the home is prepared in advance. This is particularly important when you are bringing home a wild canine. Even if it is a puppy, you need to have the outside enclosures ready because your puppy will not stay small long.

If you have not deduced this by now, let us be clear. Wild canines and their crosses are not apartment-friendly animals. They need room to live. Dumping them in an apartment and leaving for hours at a time will result in a destructive wild canine or cross that is headed for a shelter and probable euthanasia.

Photo Courtesy of Bianca and Thomas Walker

CHAPTER 6   Preparing Your Home for Your Wild Canine

Outside Issues

Your wild canine will need an approved enclosure. Have this completed before you bring home the animal. If a wild canine is legal in your location, they may have specific requirements for enclosures. Find out and follow these exactly. If you are adopting from a wild canine rescue, they may require a home visit before you bring home an animal.

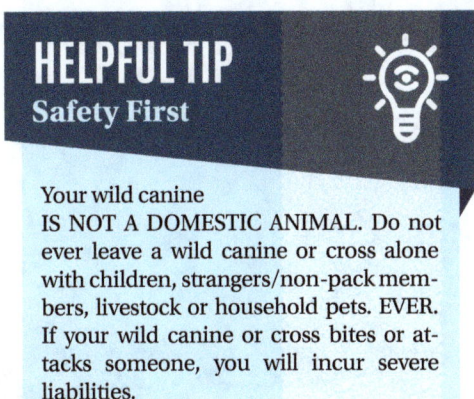

HELPFUL TIP
Safety First

Your wild canine IS NOT A DOMESTIC ANIMAL. Do not ever leave a wild canine or cross alone with children, strangers/non-pack members, livestock or household pets. EVER. If your wild canine or cross bites or attacks someone, you will incur severe liabilities.

If you plan to turn your wild canine loose in your back yard, your animal will most likely escape over the fence. A six-foot fence will not keep a dingoX, wolf dog, or coydog in your yard. If your wild canine escapes, there may be legal issues in your near future. Having an approved, appropriate structure ready for your new family member will make the transition easier.

If the animal is not legal in your state, do not get one. If you are caught, the minimum consequence will be rehoming the animal or surrendering it to a shelter. There may be fines as well. Hiding a wild canine from the authorities is not healthy for your wild canine. One very sad story from W.O.L.F. involved a wolf dog kept in a tiny dark enclosure for years so the neighbors would not find out. The mental and emotional toll on the wolf dog was severe. If you truly love the wild aspect of wolves, love them enough to keep them properly or better yet, allow them to live wild.

Chaining any animal is wrong. Chaining a wild canine is particularly heinous. If your location does not have requirements for housing a wild canine, you really must either meet enclosure requirements from another state or at bare minimum, provide an enclosed, covered, hard-floored run with a covered kennel to rest and get out of the weather.

We assume that you want a house dog and are not planning to leave your dog outside with no human interaction. If this is your plan, these are not the right dogs for you. In fact, if you don't want to engage with your animal at all, I would encourage you not to get any type of dog, wild or otherwise. Dogs of all varieties seem to need human interaction. Dumping them in a backyard is just not fair to them and will leave you with a bored, destructive animal.

Photo Courtesy of Terri Martin

Current Pets and Livestock

Adding a new dog to your collection of animals can be very difficult, or it can be simple. It depends on the personalities involved. Make sure all pets have age-appropriate vaccinations and are wormed.

W.O.L.F. keeps its wolf dogs in small packs. The most common pack structure is two neutered males and one spayed female. Most of the time, two females result in squabbling unless the wolves are littermates.

> **HELPFUL TIP**
> **Have Everything Ready**
>
> It is important to prepare for your wild canine or cross to enter your house. Before you bring home a wild canine or cross, find a vet who will care for it. Find a trainer who specializes in positive reinforcement trainer and will accept a wild canine. Have their outdoor containment system ready, follow regulations exactly, and always check your state/provincial/territorial laws as well as local and county ordinances.

Remember that you are adding an animal with an extremely high prey drive to your family. All wild canines have a high prey drive and they always will. Even well-fed captive coyotes at the Colorado Wolf and Wildlife Rescue quickly eliminate any catchable visitors including cats, mice, and birds.

Puppies have the best chance of learning to live with other animals, but the temptation will always be there. The more wild genes your pup has, the higher the prey drive.

"A common phone call goes like this... we got a wolf dog, and it loved our (domestic) dog. But yesterday, our wolf killed the other dog. We just don't understand..."

Sue Weidel, W.O.L.F.

Livestock is another concern. If you or a neighbor has horses, sheep, cattle, or similar animals, decide if you really want to add an animal that is perfectly capable of bringing down any of those animals. Just remember that your wolf, coyote, dingo, or cross will view livestock as potential prey. There is not much difference between an elk and a cow or a wallaby and a sheep in a wolf or dingo's eyes. While any dog is capable of attacking livestock, certain dogs, like wild canines, will bear a greater share of suspicion if the neighbor's sheep or chickens turn up dead.

Photo Courtesy of Jason Ryan

Interestingly, the captive wolves at W.O.L.F. ignore horses, cattle, and other animals on the other side of their fenced enclosures. The domestic animals return the favor. The wolves are also not interested in healthy individuals. An injured or young target might prove more attractive.

However, these wolves are not in a situation where they can harass, or appear to harass, livestock. Every state has laws about dogs that harass livestock. In Wyoming, for instance, a dog can legally be shot on sight for the possibility that it may harass livestock. If your dog kills or injures livestock, you are liable for damages. The same laws apply to wildlife, particularly game animals. We will quote a few of those laws in the next chapter.

CHAPTER 6 Preparing Your Home for Your Wild Canine

Children

Children and dogs can be a wonderful thing. On the other hand, children and wild canines are a recipe for disaster. Older, more self-sufficient children who respect animals will do far better than time-intensive infants, toddlers, or tweens who need constant attention or rides everywhere. Your pack-oriented dog wants to be with you. Leaving them alone for hours at a time is not healthy for them.

If you have more than one dog, does your child run the risk of triggering pack behavior by running and screaming? The unfortunate truth is that people have discovered that their dog may love their child (or cat), but when the dog is in a pack or with friends, they can forget and mob mentality – when individuals lose individual reasoning power and are guided by instinct-rules – and the child (or cat) may die.

Photo Courtesy of Christian Coombe

Pack mentality in domesticated dogs has been responsible for many injuries and deaths for children and family pets. A wild canine has an even stronger prey drive and pack mentality. If your wild canine or cross forgets and hunts down a small child, there will be severe legal penalties for both you and your pets. The emotional and mental tolls on everyone involved will be equally severe.

One wolf dog at W.O.L.F. was surrendered because the owner attempted to have the wolf dog and a day care in the same building. Just as domestic dogs will bite hands reaching through car windows or fence slats, you run at least the same risk, if not a higher risk, with a wild canine or cross. These animals are immensely more powerful than a domestic dog and capable of causing far more damage.

If you vacation a lot or travel for work, think very hard before you bring a wild canine or primitive into your home. These animals need attention. In fact, think really hard before you adopt any animal that requires human interaction.

Photo Courtesy of Kylie Settler

CHAPTER 6 Preparing Your Home for Your Wild Canine

Photo Courtesy of
Michelle Proulx
W.O.L.F., Sanctuary, Colorado

Training Classes

Puppy classes and dog classes are extremely important. Choose a dog trainer carefully. Your trainer MUST understand wild canine behavior and accept a wild canine into training. Some may not do so because of liability issues. The less wolf your wolf dog has, the easier it will be to find a trainer. High content wolf dogs need specialized training.

Your wild canine will not respond well to heavy-handed or aggressive training, so avoid Cesar Millan- or schutzhund-style training. Look for a trainer who uses positive reinforcement–based training techniques.

You also will not be able to send your dog to a trainer. The trainer is not a pack member, and your wild canine will be very unhappy away from home.

The Short Version

- Have an approved or adequate enclosure ready BEFORE you bring home a wild canine or cross.
- Children, pets, and livestock will present additional challenges when adopting a wild canine or cross.
- You need a trainer who understands wild canines and crosses and how to train them. A heavy-handed trainer is not appropriate for a wild canine.

CHAPTER 7
Preparing Your Home for Your Primitive Dog

A lot of people go, "Well, I'll get a dog because I have a kid and a kid needs a dog." And it doesn't work out for that dog and the dog is on the street.

Betty White, actress

Photo Courtesy of Cori Ludemann

A primitive dog requires preparation similar to bringing home any dog. The more ready you are for the new dog, the more successful the first few weeks will be. If you are bringing home an adult or a teen primitive, be prepared for anxiety, especially one that was wild or feral before you acquired it. They've lost their pack and do not know where they fit into yours. Patience will make all the difference in how well and quickly your new dog adapts.

Since you have owned dogs before, you probably already know about poisonous plants, dog-proofing the house, and the importance of having food and sleeping spaces ready. If you have not owned a dog before and have gotten an unexpected primitive, please pick up a guidebook for new owners in addition to this book. What follows are some primitive dog specific preparations.

Outside Issues

Take the time to check your yard or open space to make sure your primitive dog will be safe. Check fences to make sure slats or links are secure. You do not want your primitive to either squeeze through missing slats or fence fight with the neighbors. Check gates and install a dog proof latch on the gate. Your primitive may be a climbing or digging escape artist. You may not know that until you bring it home, so be prepared to modify your yard as necessary.

The breed is crazy smart and athletic. My middle Xolo clears a 6-foot fence with no issue. My oldest respects the fence and won't bother, but he tried to climb a tree after a cat and got pretty high before I was able to grab him.

Lisa Rhoades Jett, Xolo owner

If you are not sure about poisonous plants, there are many online references. There are too many in each region to comprehensively cover them all. Your extension agent, gardening club, or college agriculture department may be able to help you identify both native and non-native indoor and outdoor plants of concern.

Current Pets and Livestock

Adding a new primitive dog to your collection of animals can be very difficult, or it can be simple. It depends on the personalities involved. Make sure all pets have age-appropriate vaccinations and are wormed.

If you are adding a primitive dog into the mix, try keeping them separate for a week to let them all get used to the idea. Then slowly introduce them using gates. Face to face introductions should take place on leashes. It may be easier to add an opposite sex dog into the mix.

If you are introducing a new dog to a cat, make sure the cat's claws are well trimmed. Cats aim for the eyes when they feel threatened. Keeping claws trimmed may help prevent your dog from being blinded.

Remember that you are adding an animal with an extremely high prey drive to your family. All primitive dogs have a high prey drive. If you have smaller animals like chickens, ducks, cats, rabbits, guinea pigs, or wing-clipped birds, you may not have them long.

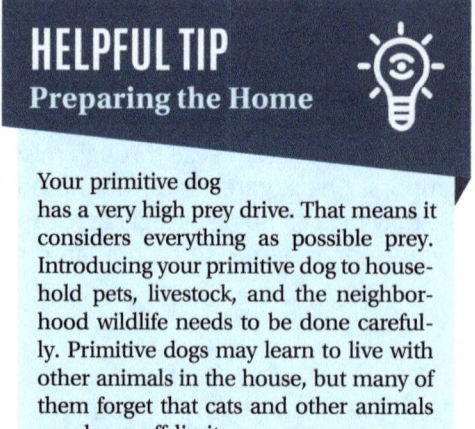

HELPFUL TIP
Preparing the Home

Your primitive dog has a very high prey drive. That means it considers everything as possible prey. Introducing your primitive dog to household pets, livestock, and the neighborhood wildlife needs to be done carefully. Primitive dogs may learn to live with other animals in the house, but many of them forget that cats and other animals are always off-limits.

Livestock is another concern. As we've stated before, every state/province has laws governing destruction of dogs that harass or kill livestock or wild animals. Your primitive might end up dead if it does so. For example, Code of Virginia § 3.1-796.116 states, "It shall be the duty of any animal warden or other officer who may find a dog in the act of killing or injuring livestock or poultry to kill such dog... Any person finding a dog committing any of the depredations...shall have the right to kill such dog on sight...."

We found that early training kept our Carolina Dog from causing such problems, although she would chase cows when allowed. Birds, mice, prairie dogs, and other small tempting targets breaking cover just under her nose was too much for her and she had a hard time stopping.

Australia also has livestock protection laws. The law in Queensland states that you can shoot a wild canine on sight, but a domestic dog is protected unless you reasonably believe the dog is attacking, or is likely to attack, your livestock and is not under someone's control.

Mules have a well-deserved reputation for disliking dogs and even killing them. Horses are capable of both killing themselves by panicking and running through fences to get away or killing a dog with a carefully placed kick. Introduce all the animals carefully.

Forcing interaction doesn't work and may never work. My two-year-old pit bull is terrified of horses but because of his breed, he does not back down. I firmly believe that he is extremely dangerous around livestock and will never allow him to interact with them.

Dogs that form packs are dangerous to livestock. Pack mentality overrides domestication. If you are trying to mix an animal with extremely high prey drives in with prey animals, you must be extremely careful. One miniature horse farm in Florida suffered the loss of two valuable therapy horses when the neighbor's dogs entered their property and maimed them so badly that the horses had to be euthanized.

CHAPTER 7 Preparing Your Home for Your Primitive Dog

Photo Courtesy of Amethea Casselman

I live on a farm. (My Xolos) are fine with animals they are raised with, but they broke into the pigs and if I hadn't been near enough to see [them], there would have been bacon for the Xolos.

Lisa Rhoades Jet, Xolo owner

Children

Photo Courtesy of Page Moore

While some children and dogs get along fine, an intolerant dog is dangerous, especially around small children who are just learning respect. A child with anger management issues can result in a dead or injured dog or a bitten child.

Long time Xolo trainer and breeder Penelope Inan commented that Xolos can be incredibly protective of their human children and take their "guardian" dog role very seriously. They do not like to have strange adults or children interacting with their children.

The ages, number, and activities of your children should play a part in the type of dog that you get. Time-intensive children and time-intensive dogs can result in destructive, ill-behaved dogs (or destructive, ill-mannered children). Consider something with lower exercise needs and less pack life requirements.

If you have more than one dog, does your child run the risk of triggering pack behavior by running and screaming? As with wild canines, a screaming child can sound like an injured animal and may trigger the prey drive. More than one dog can definitely trigger that response.

(My Xolo) picks and chooses who he likes and who he doesn't. He gets along with most animals he encounters and absolutely loves respectful children.

Kayla Marie Kolberg, Xolo owner

CHAPTER 7   Preparing Your Home for Your Primitive Dog

Training Classes

Puppy and dog classes are especially important for your primitive. You will get the help and support from a professional to understand your dog. Your dog will get socialization and learn dog manners. We'll discuss socialization in the next chapter, but it is the difference between a happy dog and happy home and a dog that gets shipped off to a shelter and probable euthanasia. Even older dogs can benefit from dog classes.

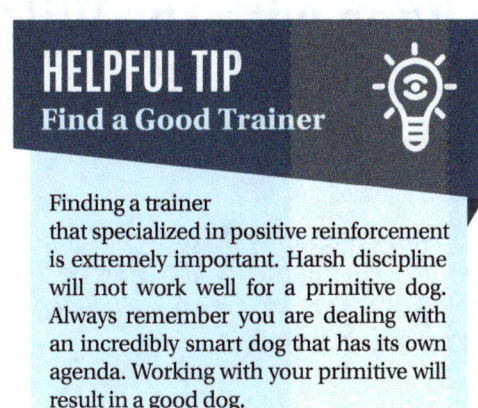

HELPFUL TIP
Find a Good Trainer

Finding a trainer that specialized in positive reinforcement is extremely important. Harsh discipline will not work well for a primitive dog. Always remember you are dealing with an incredibly smart dog that has its own agenda. Working with your primitive will result in a good dog.

Choose a dog trainer carefully. Your primitive dog will not respond well to heavy-handed or aggressive training. Use only trainers who specialize in positive reinforcement training. There are also people who specialize in training primitive dogs. Though there may not be any in your area, the internet is a wonderful tool, and you can find primitive dog training sites to help.

Check the trainer's credentials and ask for references. Sending your dog to a trainer will result in a well-trained dog for your trainer, not you. You and your dog need to train together.

As we've discussed before, training your primitive is more about teamwork. Your trainer needs to understand that and to know how to build that relationship.

The Short Version

- Primitives have high prey drives and may not fit in well with your pets or livestock.
- Pick a dog that fits in well with your family and their needs.
- Find a trainer who is used to working with primitives. If you cannot find one, go for a trainer who uses positive training techniques.

CHAPTER 8
Living with the Wild Canine or Primitive Dog

Other dogs may do their jobs in their own unique and perfectly wonderful ways, but there will always be that dog that no dog will replace, the dog that will make you cry even when it's been gone for more years than it could ever have lived.

Meghan Daum, author

Standing by Your Expectations

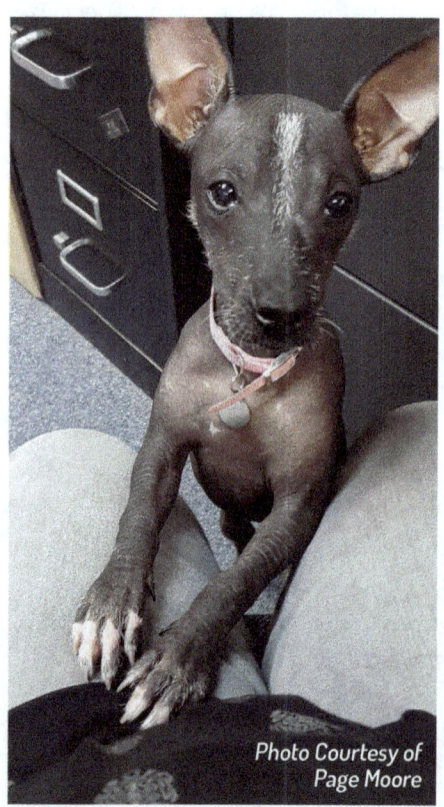

Photo Courtesy of Page Moore

Since the target audience for this book is experienced dog owners, we are going to skip the sit-down-stay training and target socialization and behaviors that commonly cause issues with primitives and wild canines. If you are considering adopting a wild canine or cross, you need to be experienced. If this is your first dog, please do not knowingly adopt one of these. Since shelters are very careful about re-homing wild crosses, you probably will never adopt one unexpectedly.

If you adopted a primitive dog by accident at a shelter where it was mislabeled, do not despair. It is possible to adjust to your dog as long as you realize what it is and how to handle its behaviors. If you feel that this dog is not right for your situation, returning it to the shelter would be the kindest act. If you de-

CHAPTER 8   Living with the Wild Canine or Primitive Dog

Photo Courtesy of Joseph Rembish

cide to keep the dog, a qualified trainer can help you through the issues and learn to work with your primitive dog or cross effectively. You may never want to go back to a domesticated dog.

Your wild canine or primitive dog wants you to be in charge, but not by being physically dominating. Rather, you need to be a good provider with logical behavior who is consistent in expectations and interactions. These animals have an innate sense of fairness and fierce loyalty that must be earned. Violating their sense of fairness can lead to power struggles. While this may sound like anthropomorphism, interaction with one will soon convince you otherwise.

For people owning a wild canine or primitive dog, these are the issues that you will probably encounter. No matter the breed or type of wild canine or primitive, every single owner has brought up the following issues. The more you work on these issues, the better socialized your dog will be, and the happier all of you will be.

What Is Socialization?

Socialization is the most important activity you can do with your new dog. Socialization helps your dog learn to enjoy interactions with other animals, strange people, new places, and different activities. The number one reason that domestic dogs are surrendered to shelter is poor socialization that has led to bad behavior. Unfortunately, about half of these unsocialized dogs will be euthanized. Socializing your dog can quite literally be the difference between life and death.

Socializing a Puppy

The closer to four weeks of age that you start socialization, the better off your primitive dog will be. The more happy, positive interactions your puppy has, the more confidence it will have. The incidence of fear biting or aggression goes way down.

Since we are gearing this book toward experienced dog owners, if you find it hard to get your pup socialized because of its instincts, you may want to consult with a professional.

Photo Courtesy of
Amethea Casselman

CHAPTER 8 Living with the Wild Canine or Primitive Dog

Photo Courtesy of Christian Coombe

Socializing an Adult

Socializing an adult is more of a challenge. It takes longer and may not be 100% effective. Just remember that the world is not the fun, shiny, new place that it is for domestic puppies. An adult dog can be socialized, but it will take time and repetition. Keep your animal safe from either acting out in fear or getting more frightened. As he starts to acclimate to new sights and sounds, add more. A professional should be able to help you socialize an older dog to the greatest extent possible for that dog.

You will have more of a challenge with a wild canine. Try to socialize within the limits of your individual's tolerance.

What Is Bad Behavior in Dogs?

Bad behavior is rooted in eight different causes: boredom, lack of exercise, lack of socialization, genetics, illness/injury, inconsistent home life, fear, and poor discipline. Bad behavior can be a combination of more than one of these.

Photo Courtesy of Christian Coombe

Boredom

Boredom is possibly the most common cause of bad behavior. Even the biggest couch potato gets bored with nothing to do and the dogs in this book are anything but couch potatoes. Letting your dog do nothing is a quick way to have shredded shoes and ripped up sheet rock.

Wild canines and primitives are extremely intelligent. One of the most important activities that occurs at wolf-dog rescues is mental stimulation. They offer toys, different foods like pumpkins, physical challenges, and games like Hide the Food.

> **HELPFUL TIP**
> **Finding the Root of the Problem**
>
> Primitives and wild canines have a well-deserved reputation for being stubborn, opinionated, tenacious and "untrainable." They are not untrainable, but they do need special positive behavior training techniques and they need to feel the training is worth their time and effort.

Mental stimulation is just as important for your primitive dog. But be aware that they like to do what they like to do, not what you might have decided to do.

Lack of Exercise

Along with boredom, add in lack of exercise. Wild canines and primitives travel long distances as they hunt and patrol their territory. You will need to simulate those distances with your wild canine. Wild and primitive dogs generally need even more exercise than the average domestic dog. If you want an active animal, primitives are great. They are always up for a hike or a walk. Obviously, dogs need exercise based on their age and physical ability, so respect those tiny puppy legs or aching senior joints.

One of my cousins owned two Huskies. In order to exercise them, she attached each via a sled harness to tires and let them run. She said it was literally the only way she could wear them out enough to sleep. She also said that many well-meaning people thought this was dog abuse. In reality, the Huskies looked forward to the challenge and waited eagerly by their tires.

Author

Lack of Socialization

Photo Courtesy of Janelle Rosenfeld

Lack of socialization is a huge problem, as we have mentioned before. A primitive requires massive amounts of socialization, early and often. Socialization with a wild canine will probably not be particularly successful. They just do not like other dogs, animals, or people.

Keep in mind that wolf pups (and presumably coyote and dingo pups) and dog puppies develop at different rates. According to Dr. Kathryn Lord, a researcher at University of Massachusetts Medical School, wolf pups develop faster than domestic puppies, and this changes their ability to form interspecies attachments.

A domesticated dog can be socialized with a mere ninety minutes of interaction between the ages of four and eight weeks. A wolf pup needs 24-hour contact before the age of three weeks and even then, there will never be the same level of attachment that there is with a domestic dog. However, taking a wolf dog pup away from its mother at less than three weeks is not advisable as the pup loses out on learning canine manners from its mother. You pretty much cannot win the wolf pup age versus socialization issue.

Colorado Wolf and Wildlife Rescue professionals have raised coyote pups from two days old. This included living in a home, being bottle fed regularly, and washed clean. If coyotes were capable of socialization, this intense level of human interaction should result in a socialized animal. However, this has never been the case. Once the coyote pup matured, it became extremely destructive, reverted to all its wild tendencies, and had to be moved into an enclosure. Coydogs can be similarly destructive and wild.

Genetics

Genetics can contribute to bad behavior as well. This plays a huge role in the wild canines and primitive dogs. In domestic dogs, you may be able to blame the parents or inbreeding. In wild canines and primitives, you can blame thousands of years of genetic shaping to survive. They are what they are.

In all probability, dogs descended from the most genetically social wolves who chose to move in with humans at the dawn of dog-human interaction. It was these social wolves that became our social dogs. The wolves who were genetically less predisposed to be social with humans stayed wild. The chances are very low that you will get a socially predisposed wolf out of a wild wolf. It may happen, but the odds are not in your favor.

> **HELPFUL TIP**
> **Socializing is the Difference Between Life and Death**
>
> Socializing is preparing your dog to be comfortable in new surroundings or situations. Poor socialization is responsible for most people dropping dogs and wild canine crosses at shelters. Every year, 80% of wolf crosses and millions of dogs are euthanized because of poor socialization.

Illness and Injury

Illness or injury can contribute to bad behavior. It is hard to be your best when you are hurting. Wolf dogs and presumably other wild canines are extremely stoic. Acting sick alerts other pack members that they may need to cull the injured animal from the pack, or that their status is open to challenge. You will not know they are hurting until they can no longer hide it. Bad behavior might be your only clue that your wild canine or primitive is in pain or is sick.

Inconsistent Home Life

Inconsistent home life is another issue that may make wild canines and primitive dogs act out. They like things just the way they are. Changing their surroundings can raise anxiety to the level of bad behavior. Moving, divorce, adding children, changing jobs, repainting your house, new furniture, traveling – these are all stressors and a sensitive wild canine or primitive may react badly.

> *(Xolos are) very, very sensitive. They're emotionally sensitive to change which can result in physical issues. Changes in the household can make them physically sick.*
>
> **Sydney Brooke Cooper, Xolo owner**

Fear

Fear is part of wild canine life. It is so basic and hardwired into mammalian subconscious that it comes with its own physiological responses, the fight or flight response that all of us know only too well.

Wild canines generally do not like human interaction and may become fearful if they cannot escape. If you've adopted a feral dog, you may have a fearful dog, more used to human cruelty than affection. Always remember that a scared dog is a biting dog. A frightened animal may become a "bad dog" out of nothing more than being in uncomfortable surroundings.

> *Working with primitive dogs has made me a better trainer. I understand the fear-aggression response in domestic dogs much more clearly.*
>
> **Cori Ludeman,
> primitive dog trainer and Carolina Dog owner**

Photo Courtesy of
Michelle Proulx
W.O.L.F., Sanctuary, Colorado

Poor Discipline

Poor discipline is a final factor. Wild canines and primitive dogs do not respond well to harsh methods. However, they need proper discipline in the form of clear expectations and consistent handling. Your wild canine or primitive is perfectly able to be well behaved as long as the discipline is presented in the proper way.

None if this is designed to excuse bad behavior in wild canines and primitive dogs. However, if you are dealing with a wild canine or primitive, you will need to factor all these reasons into your dog's behavior.

Photo Courtesy of Rob Perez

How to Properly Correct Your Wild Canine or Primitive Dog

We've mentioned several times that physical punishment is not a good way to deal with any dog, but very particularly with wild and primitive dogs. Closer examination of wolf behaviors is very enlightening. The idea of an alpha male and alpha female as tyrants who rule their pack with an iron paw, based on Konrad Lorenz's pre–World War I German military dog training, is not correct.

Instead the alpha male and female are the single breeding pair in a pack. David Mech, a wolf expert, details how the "alpha" wolves set fairly loose rules, and the other wolves live within those rules. Any squabbles result from young pups challenging lower-ranked wolves or when there is an opening in the pack structure that needs to be filled. Mech has found that only when forced into artificial packs or with multiple breeding pairs do leadership contests occur. These artificial packs can very easily be extended to include human packs.

In 2010, Italian researcher Roberto Bonanni studied a free-ranging twenty-seven-feral-dog pack. He found that leadership was very fluid, and six dogs generally served as leaders. However, over time, at least half of the dogs took leadership roles. His conclusion was that the pack leader was the dog who could offer the best leadership at the specific time.

With both these situations in mind, common "training" punishments like hitting or kicking; electric shock; physically forcing a dog into an alpha roll; shouting; threatening stares; growls; and shaking are not effective. Dr. Meghan Herron of the University of Pennsylvania's School of Veterinary Medicine found that physical punishment resulted in forty-three percent of dogs increasing their aggressive responses. She found that the most effective punishment without aggressive response was a "schhht" sound correction, followed by a leash correction (a sharp single tug on the leash). Hitting and kicking resulted in forty-three percent of dogs showing an aggressive response, while alpha rolls trigger an aggressive response in thirty-one percent of dogs.

Wild canines and primitive dogs are far more sensitive than the average domestic dog and far more status conscious. Using harsh techniques may result in negative results. Often something as simple as a frown will be effective to curb bad behavior in your wild canine or primitive dog. Your wild or primitive dog will respond much more quickly to positive reinforcement than it will to physical punishment.

How to Crate Train

Crates are very important to your wild canine or primitive dog. These animals need a safe, enclosed place to sleep or rest. They tend to be more anxious about noise and excitement than domesticated dogs.

Give your dog a safe place to hide, such as a crate covered with a heavy blanket and lined with a soft washable bed. It is far better than your dog hiding in your closet and shedding their hair all over your clothes!

Teach children and visitors that the crate is your animal's safe place, and they are to be left strictly alone when in the crate. Your wolf or wolf dog probably will not allow visitors in the house, so if you want visitors, you will need a safe enclosure for your animals well away from your visitors.

Two important crating considerations need to be discussed. First, if you are constantly leaving your wild canine or primitive dog in a crate for hours, you will have a neurotic, destructive animal. If you are leaving them alone for hours at a time, these are not the right dogs for you. Second, the crate is a safe place, not a jail. Let your dog use it as a safe place.

Chewing

Chewing is normal. In fact, chewing is absolutely necessary to healthy jaws. As mentioned before, coyotes fed a soft diet lose the ability to eat regular coyote food. This explains why a coyote living off trash cannot be relocated to a wilder setting.

Photo Courtesy of Tahoe Beetschen

Your primitive or wild canine loves chewing. Give them lots of cured bones that were not processed in China, Mexico, Brazil, or Colombia. Unfortunately, Chinese-made treats have been directly associated with a very rare and deadly liver disorder called Fanconi's Syndrome. Chinese treats tend to be very high in the pesticide phorate. While phorate is a known neurotoxin, there is no known connection to liver disorders. However, dogs fed treats from China often quickly develop liver disorders.

Treats from Mexico, Brazil, and Colombia are tainted with a quaternary ammonium compound mixture used to cleaning food processing equipment. This mixture causes vomiting and diarrhea in dogs. Err on the side of caution and feed food and treats made in your country.

If you are feeding the BARF diet, follow their recommendations about bones. DO NOT GIVE chicken bones or pork bones. Cooked chicken and all pork bones splinter easily and can pierce your dog's mouth, throat, and digestive system. This can result in death or expensive surgeries.

Rawhide should be provided with caution. Dogs like to chew on rawhide until it is soft and soggy. That creates a terrific breeding ground for bacteria that can make your dog, or even you if you touch it, very sick. Some dogs are very sensitive to the chemicals used to create rawhide. If your dog swal-

Photo Courtesy of Jason Stockmyer

lows a hunk of rawhide, they can end up with esophagus or stomach blockages. Those can be fatal or require expensive surgery.

Raw bones can also be problematic. They offer nutrients not available in smoked bones and are less likely to splinter than smoked bones. However, raw bones are a great place to breed bacteria. They are also messy on flooring and leave behind food scraps that go rancid very quickly. If you offer a raw bone, only allow your dog to have it for about 10 to 15 minutes a day. Remove it safely when your dog is distracted or directly if it is not food aggressive, and then store it in the fridge. Toss it after three days of chewing. Dogs with pancreatitis or nervous stomachs should not have fatty bones.

If your dog chews on something off limits, take it away calmly and safely and immediately give them an appropriate toy. Your wild canine may take exception if you do not outrank them, so be careful.

Growling and Barking

Growling is your dog's first verbal indication that it is unhappy or uncomfortable. Dogs growl to communicate that they are not comfortable with their surroundings. They will growl in fear, in possession aggression, territory defense, or pain. A growling dog may very quickly become a biting dog. Scolding or punishing your dog for growling only makes a silent biter. Disengage immediately and show your displeasure by not responding to your dog's overtures.

Wolves and coyotes will bare their teeth. Backing down means you lose. Engaging them means you lose. Putting a positive spin on this is just not possible. If you put your wild canine in a position where it challenges you, you will probably never regain the upper hand.

Barking is your dog's way of communicating over distance, initiating play, warning of danger, threatening, or because it is curious or bored. Do not yell at a barking dog. Your dog thinks you are barking too, so whatever is going on needs more barking.

Howling is a normal part of coyote, wolf, and Spitz-type primitive behavior. If you are planning to get one, your neighbors may take exception to nightly serenades. Our neighbors have huskies. They will spend a good part of each day howling while their owners are gone. It is fine the first time, but daily howling sessions get very annoying.

Aggression

Because wolves, coyotes, and dingoes are very territorial, they can be extremely aggressive when newcomers enter their territory. They are also very wary of humans, especially when the animal is wild caught. Aggression and fear-aggression will always be a concern for a wild canine.

Primitives are also territorial. Whether or not you can add another animal or even be around other animals depends on how wild your primitive was when acquired, the unique personalities involved, and how well socialized the primitive was in the first place.

Primitive dogs take food or other scarce resource (toys) squabbles seriously – even if there are plenty of toys or food. Most domestic dogs will squabble and then disengage. Primitive dogs may not. This was one issue I ran into with my Carolina Dog and my former bait dog. Neither was able to back down and their fights were terrifying. You may need a professional to help with an un- or under-socialized adult wild canine or primitive dog.

Digging

Wild canines, crosses, and primitives like to dig. They will dig holes of all sizes in your yard or garden. If you must have a pristine golf course yard, you will not like these dogs. They will not stop digging. Do not get one if you cannot tolerate dens and pits all over your yard.

You may need to install escape-proof fences to stop your wild or primitive dog from digging out or climbing out. As we have noted in the section on wild canine housing, you may need to have very specific enclosures to prevent digging and climbing escapes.

Photo Courtesy of Kylie Settler

Separation Anxiety

Separation anxiety is a common reason dogs end up at shelters. A dog with separation anxiety is destructive when left alone for any time. Keep in mind that if you choose to own a pack-oriented dog like a wolf dog, you may encounter separation anxiety.

Our current pit bull has separation anxiety to the point that you cannot have a closed door between you and him. He either goes everywhere with us or spends limited time kenneled. It was also the reason his previous owners left him in a shelter.

Running Away

A bored, under-exercised, curious wild canine or primitive may decide to take off for the day. Every wild canine cross owner knows crosses like to roam.

Not all primitives are runners, but ones that are can be problems. Your dog may be hit by a car, get into fights, or forget the way home. Always make certain your dog is in a secure yard or enclosure and on leash when out of your yard.

It is possible to prevent bad behaviors in primitive dogs. As long as you understand what they need and provide it, you can have a very well-mannered dog. It may be a bit harder with coyotes and dingoes as they are less interested in being socialized. If you need help, find someone who can guide you and your dog. It is worth the money and the effort.

The Short Version

- Bad behavior is rooted in eight different causes: boredom, lack of exercise, lack of socialization, genetics, illness/injury, inconsistent home life, fear, and poor discipline.
- Primitives need as much socializing as possible. Socializing the wild canine may not be particularly successful.
- Primitives and wild canines do not do well with aggressive physical punishment or training.

CHAPTER 9
Traveling with Wild Canines and Primitives

I desperately want a dog, but I've been told I travel too much, and I'm not allowed to have a dog.

Victoria Pratt, actress

Traveling while you own a wild canine or cross is going to present you with some issues. Traveling with primitives will meet with the same requirements and challenges that any other dog does.

Photo Courtesy of Terri Martin

CHAPTER 9   Traveling with Wild Canines and Primitives

Kenneling

We've mentioned several times that wild canines and their crosses are very pack oriented. Leaving them alone for long periods of time is not healthy for them.

Professional kennels may be reluctant to accept wild canines and their crosses. These animals do not like to be away from their pack and stable surroundings and may react badly. Bringing someone in to take care of them may be equally problematic. Non-pack members are often not welcome on their territory and your wild canine or cross may not tolerate that person in their kennel or home.

Kenneling your primitive is up to that specific dog and its personality. Some will handle it well, some will not.

Our wolf dog was at (a vet facility) when one of the vet techs went into the enclosure with him. She was snapped at. Luckily, it didn't break the skin so she didn't have to report it to her supervisor – she just told us – because the wolf dog would have been put down immediately had the facility known.

former Wyoming wolf dog owners

Flying

Flying a wild animal or cross, even as a pet, is difficult. According to American Airlines, you may transport a wolf or coyote via plane to and from states where it is legal to own them. However, they must be shipped as Zoo to Zoo or Zoo to Preserve. Without specialized arrangements at both ends, shipping a wolf or coyote may be extremely difficult.

According to Qantas, it is possible to ship a dingo domestically, but it must be in an approved crate and can be refused transport

> **HELPFUL TIP**
> **Traveling On an Airplane**
>
> Airplane travel with any sort of dog is a challenge. Always contact the individual airlines to find out their requirements. If you are traveling with a wild canine or cross, the restrictions will be more restrictive and may require permits from the airline, any ports of call and even to be shipped from zoo to zoo.

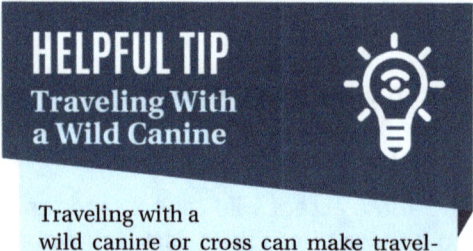

HELPFUL TIP
Traveling With a Wild Canine

Traveling with a wild canine or cross can make traveling very difficult traveling may be very difficult. You may need special permits to cross state/provincial lines, hotels may have breed or size restrictions, and boarding facilities may refuse to house your wild canine. Make sure you do plenty of research before traveling with (or without) your wild canine.

if it is actively trying to destroy the crate. Qantas ships pets domestically, as solo travelers, and internationally. They will not transport "fighting" dogs and snub-nosed dogs. Qantas may also refuse to ship animals that show aggression or who are attempting to destroy their cages.

Primitives have no restrictions, so travel is based on your individual dog. Depending on the size of your dog, you will probably have to ship it. Only dogs that can fit under your seat can travel in the cabin (except for service animals).

Within the United States, only fully weaned animals at least ten weeks old can be shipped domestically. They must be at least sixteen weeks old before traveling from other countries into the United States and at least fifteen weeks old before traveling to Europe. Most domestic airlines will not allow warm-blooded animals on flights over twelve hours. Canada and Australia have very similar regulations.

The International Pet and Animal Transportation Association is an excellent resource for finding domestic and international shipping companies that will ship wild canines or crosses. They can help find shippers who will transport animals for long-haul flights. They also maintain a list of known pet scammers' emails or commonly used names for you to double check before buying a pup online.

After several well-publicized tragedies involving shipped pets, airlines are now taking the care and handling of pets more seriously. In order to ship an animal, you will need to comply with a number of regulations. In general, you will need a health certificate completed within ten days. The health certificate must include the shipper's name and address, any tag numbers or tattoos, a record of all inoculations, and the vet's signature.

You will be required to confirm that your pet has been fed and watered within four hours of check-in. You will also need to supply food for the next twenty-four hours, even if your dog will arrive before that much time has elapsed. Tape a baggie full of food to the kennel. You do not want the baggage handler to open the kennel so make it easy for them to feed your dog without opening the door at all.

CHAPTER 9   Traveling with Wild Canines and Primitives

Vets may recommend tranquilizers, and you will have to provide written consent from your vet. High altitude may affect how tranquilizers work and how long they last. If you can, do not tranquilize your pet. In most cases, the airline will not allow handlers to administer medications, so if your dog requires regular medication for health concerns, you may either need to leave it at home or find another means of transporting it.

You will also have to contend with temperature restrictions. Airlines will not accept pets at ground temperatures over 80°F (27°C) or below 20°F (-7°C). We shipped our Carolina Dog on a direct flight from Atlanta to Denver. It took some coordination on both ends and a lot of driving. We were almost unable ship her because the temperature in Atlanta was climbing toward 80°F. She was put on the airplane at 79°F.

International travel is even trickier and has many more requirements. The representatives recommended contacting the individual airline as well as border control officials in the departing and arriving countries.

Photo Courtesy of Terri Martin
Photo by Carl Webb

Hotel Stays

Hotel stays can also be an issue. Many hotels restrict the size of animal they will allow in the room and most wolves and wolf crosses exceed the size limit.

As with all dogs, do not leave them unsupervised in the room. I highly recommend keeping any dog leashed when opening the door. Your animal will be less likely to either terrify room service or escape.

Crossing State or International Boundaries

This is a very sticky point. Crossing state lines with a wolf or coyote or cross may require a permit. Some states, like Kentucky, limit the amount of time the animal can stay in the state. Others, like Alabama, require a permit to pass through the state with a coyote but the animal cannot remain in the state for any length of time. Other states/provinces, including Alaska, Manitoba, and Nova Scotia, do not allow ownership of wolves or coyotes or crosses and thus you cannot take yours into those locations. In Wyoming, if you move to the state with a wolf or coyote or cross, you will be required to rehome the animal to a rescue or state where the animal is legal.

Obviously, if you are planning a trip with your wild canine or cross, you need to contact each state/province individually to check their requirements.

Photo Courtesy of Christian Coombe

CHAPTER 9   Traveling with Wild Canines and Primitives

Shipping wolves, coyotes and dingoes internationally are subject to importation laws on departure and arrival. In some cases, their crosses will be regulated as "wild animals" as well. Always check with the shipper and border control at ports of call, even if you are just passing through that country.

Internationally, your primitive will be treated like a regular domestic dog and may need proof of rabies or other requirements required by the country you are traveling to.

Photo Courtesy of Rae Druiff-Fick

The Short Version

- Kenneling a wild canine depends on the kennel. A wild canine will probably not be particularly happy in a kennel.
- Flying depends on your dog's age and personality, the breed, and where you are going. Always contact border control at all points of entry if you are traveling with a wild canine.
- If you are traveling interstate or interprovince, make certain your wild canine will not be confiscated and possibly euthanized.

Photo Courtesy of Terri Martin

THE FINAL HOWL

When you adopt a dog, you have a lot of very good days and one very bad day.

W. Bruce Cameron, author

If you've been considering getting a wild canine, you should now have enough information to make an informed decision. If you've fallen in love with a primitive dog, by now you should know exactly what you are getting and how to interact with these very special dogs.

Photo Courtesy of Jilliyn Cunningham

When I started writing this book, I began by asking former wild canine owners and my long-suffering vet for permission to interview them. Here's how every conversation went...

Me: I'm doing a book on owning wolf dogs. Can I talk to you about your experience?

Them, after long suspicious silence: You are not planning to get one, are you?

Me: Nope, my pit bull is enough for me.

Them: *relieved laughter*

That mindset became the basis for the wild canine and cross portions of the book.

Every single friend, primitive dog owner, wolf dog owner, and rescue professional summed up their experience with wild canines and primitive dogs in exactly the same way:

1. These are the best dogs ever.
2. The experience was truly amazing.
3. I would do it again if only I was younger.
4. These are not the right dogs for everyone.

Photo Courtesy of Christian Coombe

When you think about all the challenges of bringing home a wild canine or primitive dog, there is a lot to consider. It is a huge responsibility. It may be the best experience in your life, but do not go into wild canines, cross or primitive dog ownership unprepared. Your choice may cost your animal his life.

If you are choosing one of these animals because of the status, the cool factor, or because your favorite TV character has one, please reread this book. I'll say it one more time. Wild canines and crosses are NOT the right pets for inexperienced dog owners and are probably not even the best pets for most experienced owners.

You will be taking home a whole tremendous amount of work. If you can work with your dog on their terms and live your life around this animal, you have a good chance of this being a successful experience.

Would I take in another Carolina Dog? In a heartbeat, until I remember how much time and effort I put into my first Carolina Dog. I just do not have the time or energy to invest and without that investment, I know that having another primitive dog would ultimately not be a positive experience.

APPENDIX 1
United States

Dingoes and dingo crosses are not legal for import. Dogs referred to as "dingoes" are generally either mislabeled Carolina Dogs or Australian cattle dogs.

Some states allow possession with permitting. HOWEVER, the permitting process is not guaranteed and may be extremely restrictive.

*** NOTE: State laws are subject to change. Always confirm BEFORE bringing home a pure or cross wild canine. ***

Table 1: List of US states indicating the legality of owning wild canines and crosses, as of April 2019.

	Wolf	Wolf cross	Coyote	Coydog
Alabama	Yes	Yes	No	No
Alaska	No	No	No	No
Arizona	Yes with permit	Yes	Yes with permit	Yes
Arkansas	Yes, with special provisions	Yes, with special provisions	Yes, with special provisions	Yes, with special provisions
California	No, unless able to comply with permitting regulations	Yes, subject to local ordinances	No	See local ordinances
Colorado	No	Yes	No	Yes
Connecticut	No	No	No	No
Delaware	Yes, with special provisions, except in New Castle or Kent County	No in New Castle County or in Kent County	No	See local ordinances
D.C.	No	No	No	No
Florida	Yes, with provisions	Yes, but if it closely resembles a wolf, it must meet provisions	Yes, with provisions	Yes, but if it closely resembles a coyote, it must meet provisions
Georgia	No	No	No	No

Appendix 1 United States

Hawaii	No	No	No	No
Idaho	Only by special permit	Yes, with provisions	Yes	Yes
Illinois	No	No	No	No
Indiana	Yes, with provisions	Yes, with provisions	Yes, with provisions	Yes, with provisions
Iowa	No, unless superseded by local officials	No, unless superseded by local officials	No, unless superseded by local officials	No, unless superseded by local officials
Kansas	Yes, with special wildlife possession permit	Yes, with receipt	Yes, with provisions	Yes, with receipt
Kentucky	No	Yes, up to 25% wolf	Yes, with special provisions	Yes
Louisiana	No	No if it resembles a wolf, unless documented	See local ordinances	See local ordinances
Maine	Yes, with provisions	Yes, with provisions	Yes, with provisions	Yes, with provisions
Maryland	No	No	No	No
Massachusetts	No	No	No	No
Michigan	No	No	Yes, with provisions	Yes, unless resembles a coyote then yes with permitting
Minnesota	Yes, with special provisions	Yes, unless local ordinances apply	No if trapped from wild	Yes
Mississippi	No	No	Yes in permitted coyote enclosures	Illegal to import
Missouri	Yes, with special provisions	Yes, with special provisions	Yes, with special provisions	Yes, with special provisions
Montana	Yes, with special provisions	Yes, with special provisions for up to 50%	Yes, with special provisions	Yes, with special provisions
Nebraska	No	Yes, unless it looks like a wolf	No	Yes, unless it looks like a coyote

State	Col1	Col2	Col3	Col4
Nevada	Yes, subject to local ordinance	Yes, subject to local ordinance	No	No
New Hampshire	No	No, but special situations may apply	Yes, with special provisions	Yes, with special provisions
New Jersey	No	Yes, with proof of cross status	No	Yes, with proof of cross status
New Mexico	No	No	No	No
New York	Yes, with permitting	Yes, with permitting	Yes, with permitting	Yes, with permitting
North Carolina	Red wolf no Gray by local ordinances	By local ordinances	No	Not if looks like a coyote
North Dakota	Yes, with special provisions	Yes, with special provisions	Yes, with special provisions	Yes, with special provisions
Ohio	Depends on local jurisdiction	Depends on local jurisdiction	Depends on local jurisdiction	Depends on local jurisdiction
Oklahoma	Yes, with breeder's license	Yes	Yes, with breeder's license	Yes
Oregon	No	Yes, with proof of cross	No	Yes, with proof of cross
Pennsylvania	Yes, with special provisions	Yes, with special provisions	Yes, with special provisions	Yes, with special provisions
Rhode Island	Yes, with special provisions	Yes, with special provisions	Yes, with special provisions	Yes, with special provisions
South Carolina	Yes, with special provisions	Yes, with special provisions	Yes, with special provisions	Yes, with special provisions
South Dakota	Yes, with special provisions	Yes, with special provisions	Yes, with special provisions	Yes, with special provisions
Tennessee	No	Yes	Yes, if adopted from a USDA-certified facility not feeding roadkill	Not recognized as a possibility
Texas	May be subject to local ordinance	Yes, subject to local ordinance	Yes, subject to local ordinance	Yes, subject to local ordinance

Utah	No	Yes, subject to local ordinance	No	Yes subject to local ordinance
Vermont	Yes, with special permitting	Yes	Yes, with special permitting	Yes
Virginia	No	Yes, subject to local ordinance	No	Yes, subject to local ordinance
Washington	No	Yes, subject to local ordinance	No	Yes, subject to local ordinance
West Virginia	No	No	No	No
Wisconsin	No	Yes, with permit, subject to local ordinances	Yes, with permit, subject to local ordinances	Unknown; see considerations
Wyoming	No	No	Yes	Yes
Am Samoa, Puerto Rico, Virgin Islands, N. Mariana Islands, Guam,	Importation not permitted	Importation not permitted	Importation not permitted	Importation not permitted

Special Considerations by State

Alabama: You may not own a coyote in Alabama. If you are driving through Alabama with a coyote legally held in another state, we can issue a permit to pass through our state but not to stay for any length of time.

We have no regulation prohibiting the ownership of wolves or wolf hybrids. That means that you can legally possess wolves and wolf hybrids in Alabama. Currently, no permit is required to possess them.

Alaska: Wolf and coyote hybrids are not allowed in the state. The native (indigenous) fish and wildlife of Alaska are a public resource. You may not cage or fence in a wild creature and try to make it your pet, even if you think it is a juvenile that has been abandoned. It is illegal for citizens to possess or export native Alaska species as pets.

Arizona: "Possession of wolves in Arizona is prohibited without a permit. They may not be imported or possessed except as otherwise permitted by the Arizona Game and Fish Commission. Under current Department of Game and Fish policy, any hybrid resulting from the cross of a wolf and a domestic dog is considered a domestic animal and not subject to the Department's jurisdiction." ARIZ. COMP. ADMIN R. & REGS. R12-4-406; R12-4-409; R12-4-417; R12-4-425; R12-4-426

Arkansas: As of 2018, A.C.A. § 20-19-401 – 408 "Under the law, a 'wolf-dog hybrid' means any animal which is publicly acknowledged by its owner as being the offspring of a wolf and domestic dog; however, no animal may be judged to be a wolf or wolf-dog hybrid based strictly on its appearance. The specific rabies vaccination requirements for wolf-dog hybrid are detailed as well as confinement requirements (i.e., specific fence dimensions)."

Up to six individual animals from the following list and taken by hand from the wild may be kept per household: coyotes with special provisions.

California: Ownership of pure wolves is illegal except by the few people qualifying for a valid permit from Fish and Game. Among the criteria for such a permit are rigid requirements for facilities and experience in raising such animals, along with approval of the USDA. "Any F1 (first) generation wolf hybrid whelped on or before February 4, 1988 may be possessed under permit from the department. No state permit is required to possess the progeny of F1 generation wolf hybrids, but cities and counties may prohibit possession or require a permit."

Colorado: "Pure wolves require commercial licensing and appropriate carnivore facilities. #1101 (A). No person shall possess, sell, acquire, purchase, broker, trade, barter or attempt to sell, acquire, purchase, broker, trade or barter live wildlife unless he first obtains a proper license as provided in this chapter. All species of wildlife listed on the license must be approved by the Division; such approval shall not be granted if the proposed wildlife is deemed to be detrimental to wild native wildlife. The Colorado Division of Wildlife does not regulate ownership of Wolf Hybrids as they are considered domestic animals."

You cannot own a coyote, but you can own a coydog.

Connecticut: "Possession of potentially dangerous animals. For the purposes of this section, the following shall be considered as potentially dangerous animals: …. the wolf and coyote …. No person shall possess a potentially dangerous animal. Any such animal illegally possessed may be ordered seized and may be disposed of as determined by the Commissioner of Environmental Protection. Any person who violates any provision of this section shall be fined not more than one hundred dollars for each offense…. A quadruped which results from the crossbreeding of any animal with one of the species listed above … shall be considered to be a quadruped of that species."

D.C.: Chapter 18. Animal Control. § 8-1808. (h)(1) "Except as provided in this subsection, no person shall import into the District, possess, display, offer for sale, trade, barter, exchange, or adoption, or give as a household pet any living member of the animal kingdom including those born or raised in captivity, except the following: domestic dogs (excluding hybrids with wolves, coyotes, or jackals)."

Delaware: "No person shall bring into this State, possess, sell or exhibit any live wild mammal or hybrid of a wild mammal ... not native to or generally found in Delaware without first securing a permit under this chapter." The regulations state: "There must be two enclosures to house a (Wolf Hybrid), a primary enclosure and a secondary enclosure. Fastening or locking devices shall be required on both the primary and the secondary enclosures and must be tamper proof from the general public. ... Individual animal permits are required for pet owners and Class (4) permits are required for breeders or exhibitors of wolves and Wolf Hybrids. "Delaware is divided into three counties and each has its own county government. The two northern most counties have passed laws stating that wolves and Wolf Hybrids are not allowed in New Castle County or in Kent County" 23.1.1.1.

It shall be unlawful to possess, buy, sell, barter, trade, or transfer any live coyote to or from another person unless permitted by the Director of the Division of Fish and Wildlife.

Florida: Wolves and Coyotes are both regulated as Class II Canidae. The hybrid rule reads as follows: "Hybrids resulting from the cross between wildlife and domestic animal, which are substantially similar in size, characteristics and behavior so as to be indistinguishable from the wild animal shall be regulated as wildlife at the higher and more restricted class of the wild parent." There is no set percentage of wolf or coyote that would cause the animal to be regulated as such.

Georgia: "Wolves, coyotes and crosses" are illegal to have in Georgia. Wolves, or other non-native to Georgia species, may pass through the state without a permit as long as they are not here for more than 24 hours and do not have contact with persons other than their owner. Native species, including the coyote, may not enter the state at all without a Wildlife Import Permit from the Georgia DNR Law Enforcement Division Special Permit Unit.

Hawaii: "Canis familiaris crossed with wolf, coyote, dingo, jackal, fox, dhole, African wild dog, Raccoon dog...are prohibited in the State of Hawaii. Since both wolves and coyotes would have to be imported, they are banned as well.

Idaho: Wolves must be permitted by the Director of the IDFG who may or may not allow the permit. Wolf crosses must be tattooed and registered with the IDFG. Coyotes and coydogs may be owned without regulation.

Illinois: The Illinois Dangerous Animals Act prohibits ownership or possession of wolves except for zoological parks, federally licensed exhibits, circuses, scientific or educational institutions, research laboratories, veterinary hospitals or animal refuges where they must be in an escape-proof enclosure. "There is no separate designation for the crossbred wolf/dog or coyote/dog mix, and as such are accepted as wolves if they are represented as wolf crossbreds." (sic). "It is no defense to a violation of Section 2 that the person violating such section has attempted to domesticate the dangerous animal." Illinois Revised Statutes, Chapter 8, paragraph 242(2).

Indiana: A Class III wild animal permit is required for each individual wolf. Additionally, a USDA permit must be possessed by the owner for each wolf. Wolf hybrids are not regulated by the state and do not require a permit. However, they have special provisions.

Coyotes are allowed to be possessed and sold in Indiana. A wild animal possession permit is required to keep a coyote as a pet in Indiana pursuant to Indiana Code (IC) 14-22-26 and 312 IAC 9-11 (Indiana Administrative Code). A game breeder's license is required to breed and sell coyotes in Indiana pursuant to IC 14-22-10 and 312 IAC 9-10-4.

Iowa: Local, municipal or county officials should be contacted for relevant regulations/ordinances which would supersede state regulations.

Kansas: A full bred wolf would require a special wildlife possession permit. Wolf/dog hybrids are legal to own without a permit – you should keep the receipt on where you obtained so that a paper trail could be followed in case there was a question.

Taking a coyote from the wild would require a hunting license and you could not sell it. A coyote/dog hybrid would not require any permit; you should keep the receipt on where you obtained so that a paper trail could be followed in case there was a question.

Kentucky: "Pursuant to KRS 150.183 and 301 KAR 2:081, wolves cannot be imported, transported, possessed or sold, except for certain educational, scientific, or research purposes approved by the commissioner." KRS Chap. 65, § 3 reads: "(1) A county, city, urban-county, or charter county may regulate or prohibit the holding of wildlife that have been identified by the Department of Fish and Wildlife Resources as inherently dangerous to human health and safety. (1) The department has declared the following species of wildlife to be inherently dangerous to human health and safety and shall establish procedures for denying a transportation permit for said wildlife ... wolf or wolf hybrids over 25% wolf."

Coyotes cannot be imported or transported through Kentucky.

Louisiana: "No person shall possess within the State of Louisiana any of the following species or its subspecies of live wild quadrupeds, domesticated or otherwise... Red wolf, Gray wolf." The prohibition against wolf-dog hybrids expired January 1, 1997; however, "persons are cautioned that local ordinances or other state regulations may prohibit possession of these animals." "An animal which appears indistinguishable from a wolf or is in any way represented to be a wolf may be considered to be a wolf in the absence of bona fide documentation to the contrary."

Coyotes and hybrids are regulated on local level.

Maine: Under Title 7, § 3907, 12-C of the Animal Laws of the State of Maine, "Dog means a member of the genus and species known as Canis familiaris or any canine, regardless of generation, resulting from the interbreeding of a member of Canis familiaris with a wolf hybrid as defined in subsection 30."

A separate definition reads "Wolf hybrid means a mammal that is the offspring of the reproduction between a species of wild canine or wild canine hybrid and a domestic dog or wild canine hybrid. Wolf hybrid includes a mammal that is represented by its owner to be a wolf hybrid, coyote hybrid, coydog or any other kind of wild canine hybrid."

"A dog or wolf hybrid must be licensed by its owner or keeper in accordance with the laws of this State." "If a person applying for a license declares that the dog is a wolf hybrid, a municipal clerk may issue a license without proof that the dog has been immunized against rabies. In accordance with subsection 5, the license issued for the dog must state that the dog is a wolf hybrid. Under the provisions of 22 MRSA Human Services, Sec. 1313-A, however, "If a domesticated wolf hybrid bites a person, an animal control officer, a local health officer, or a game warden may immediately kill, or order killed that animal without destroying the head."

A law passed in 2011 is attempting to eliminate ownership of wolf dogs: Under Maine's law, people are prohibited from acquiring wolf dogs unless they have a permit issued by the Department of Inland Fisheries and Wildlife to possess wildlife in captivity.

Maryland: "A person or incorporated or unincorporated organization may not harbor or move within Maryland any live wolves or hybrids, for which there is no U.S.D.A. certified vaccine against rabies, without first having obtained a permit from the Service."

Maryland Criminal Law 10-621 that prohibits the ownership of coydogs (coyote hybrids). (1) A person may not import into the State, offer for sale, trade, barter, possess, breed, or exchange a live... member of the dog family other than the domestic dog; or hybrid of a member of the dog family and a domestic dog.

Massachusetts: Permits for wild animals: You will not be issued a permit for keeping a wild animal as a pet. The Code of Massachusetts Regulations (321 CMR 2.12) describes these regulations in full. Any animal listed in ... any category of federal endangered species law... may not be possessed without a permit (includes wolves).

Chapter 131: Section 77A. Wild canine and felid hybrids, Section 77A. No person shall possess, sell, trade, breed, import, export or release a wild canine hybrid except as otherwise provided by rules and regulations of the division. Any mammal which is the offspring of the reproduction between any species of wild canine or hybrid wild canine and a domestic dog or hybrid wild canine, or is represented by its owner to be a wolf hybrid, coyote hybrid, coy dog or any other kind of wild canine hybrid...shall be considered to be wild mammals and subject to the provisions of this chapter.

Michigan: Wolves and wolf dog crosses are not legal to possess in this state.

The Michigan Department of Natural Resources (MDNR) does not have any regulations on the ownership of a coyote/dog cross. However, the MDNR does require a permit for holding game in captivity for game animals purchased from a breeder. That means if a coydog looks mostly like a coyote it would require a permit. If the animal looks mostly like a dog it would not require a permit and it would then be regulated by the Michigan Department of Agriculture's Animal Industry Division.

Minnesota: It is illegal to own a wolf without a permit. It is illegal in Minnesota to possess any animal taken from the wild, unless you are a licensed rehabilitator. You could not trap a coyote and keep it as a pet. Theoretically, if you could find one from a licensed breeder, you would be able to have that, but you would have to have paperwork to show where it came from. Check with the Board of Animal Health to find out what their regulations would be. You need a veterinarian's certificate showing that the coyote was healthy and up to date on shots. Check with city, county, or any other rule-making authority that could prohibit you from keeping an exotic pet.

There are not any Minnesota State Laws regarding the breeding of a wolf-dog hybrid. A wolf-dog hybrid would be considered a domestic dog and the DNR does not have any authority over possession or ownership of these types of animals. There is one Game and Fish law that, M.S. 97B.645 limits the release of any wolf-dog hybrids. A coyote-dog would also be considered a domestic dog.

Mississippi: "It is unlawful for any person to import, transfer, sell, purchase or possess any wild animal classified as inherently dangerous by law or regulation unless that person holds a permit or is exempt from holding a permit." "The following wild animals are classified as animals inherently dangerous to humans ... wolves, jackals and dingoes; all species, including crosses between wolves and domestic animals." Prior to the issuance of a permit, the applicant must provide proof of liability insurance.

Live nuisance animals may not be possessed except 1. Coyotes in permitted coyote enclosures; ... The coyote/dog hybrid issue is not defined in regulations. However, the only way you could really have one here would be through the chance mating of dog and wild coyote since there is no provision to have breeding facilities for such and it would not be legal to import one from elsewhere.

Missouri: "Any person holding wildlife in captivity in any manner shall have in his/her possession the prescribed permit or evidence of exemption." "Wolves and Wolf hybrids are considered Class II wildlife and there are minimum containment specifications and recordkeeping requirements." With the Class I Wildlife Breeder permit you can have Coyote Hybrids.

Montana: The regulations define "wolf" as "any canine which is one-half or more wolf. All 50% or greater crosses and pure wolves are required to be tattooed and registered."

Coyotes and presumably coyote hybrids could be owned as a pet provided the person notifies the department and gets a tattoo number assigned and applied to the animal.

Nebraska: "No person shall keep the following in captivity in Nebraska nor will a permit be issued: wolf...."

In addition, wild coyotes cannot be captured and possessed, and they cannot be imported. A person cannot own a coyote in Nebraska. Coydogs would be considered dogs, similar to wolf/dog hybrids.

Nevada: According to NAC 503.110 "Except as otherwise provided in this section and NAC 504.486, the importation, transportation or possession of the following species of live wildlife or hybrids thereof, including viable embryos or gametes, is prohibited: Coyote (Canis latrans)." Because the coydog is a hybrid of the coyote it would illegal to own.

However, other exotic animals including wolves may be possessed without a permit or license. NEV. ADMIN. CODE ch. 503, §110; ch. 503, §140; ch. 504, §488 Wolf hybrids are not regulated at a state level.

New Hampshire: It is unlawful for persons to possess exotic animals, such as wolves, unless they are exhibitors. N.H. REV. STATE ANN.

§207:14 and N.H. CODE ADMIN. R Fis §802.01, §804.01, §804.02, §804.03, §804.04, §804.05,

A person must possess a permit to possess any live wildlife, or their hybrid, designated as controlled, including coyotes

New Jersey: It is unlawful for persons to possess a potentially dangerous species as a "pet." Potentially dangerous species include Carnivora (nondomestic dogs) N.J. ADMIN. CODE tit. 7, §25-4.8 and §25-4.9

Hybrids are not currently regulated in New Jersey, so it is legal to possess them. However, proof that the animal is indeed a hybrid is required.

New Mexico: "Except as otherwise provided in the Wildlife Conservation Act (17-2-37 - 17-2-46 NMSA 1978), it is unlawful for any person to take, possess, transport, export, sell or offer for sale, or ship any threatened or endangered species or subspecies, or any restricted species. The gray wolf (Canis lupus) is listed as an endangered species in New Mexico. Wolf crosses, coyotes and coydogs may not be possessed."

New York: Dangerous Wildlife License Statutory Authority: ECL 3-0301, 11-0325, 11-0511 and 6 NYCRR Part 175 and Part 180

No person may possess, release, transport, import or export, or cause to be released, transported, imported, or exported, except under permit from the department, any of the following live wildlife: Any Wolf/Dog hybrid, Any animal, whose overall appearance makes it difficult, or impossible to distinguish from a wolf (Canis lupis), or a coyote (Canis latrans).

New York Environmental Conservation Law Section 11-0103 - Definitions.

North Carolina: "Possession of eastern timber wolves or red wolves (100% purebred stock) would require a wildlife captivity license. The Commission does not recognize wolf-hybrids as wild animals." N.C. SESS. LAWS §153A-131 and §160A-187; N.C. ADMIN. CODE tit. 2, r. 52B.0212. Coyotes and coydogs that look like coyotes are prohibited.

North Dakota: The regulations describe three categories of animals including category 3 – those species determined by the board to pose special concerns, including species which are inherently dangerous or environmentally hazardous (such as wolves and coyotes and hybrids). There are specific licensing requirements for category 2 and 3 species. NDAC 48.1-09-01-01 - 48.1-09-06-01, 2017

Ohio: Ownership of wolves, coyotes, and hybrids fall under the jurisdiction of the local dog warden in the state of Ohio, however according to state law, no person shall possess a dangerous wild animal on or after January 1,

2014. Includes wolves but not hybrids. O.H. REV. CODE §1533.71; and §935. O.H. ADMIN CODE 901:1-2 and 901:1-4.

Oklahoma: It is illegal to keep, possess, own, harbor or exhibit any animal wild by nature (wolves and coyotes) except as an exhibition complying with all aspects of federal laws and regulations and Oklahoma laws and regulations applicable to exhibition of animals wild by nature.

A non-commercial breeder's license is not required to own a single pure wolf; however, the animal must be purchased from a commercial breeder and a sales receipt must be kept to prove origin. If two or more animals are owned, then a non-commercial breeder's license must be purchased. If two or more wolves are owned and bred for resale, then a commercial breeder's license must be purchased. Pure wolves are also regulated by the federal agencies. OKLA. STAT. Tit. 29, §4-107 A wolf/dog hybrid is considered a domestic animal and not wildlife

Oregon: Pureblood wolfs are not legal to own in Oregon and if ODFW questions the purity it is up to the owner to provide proof that it is a hybrid (Oregon Administrative Rules (OAR) Division 44). Hybrid wolves are under the authority of Oregon Dept. of Agriculture (Oregon Revised Statutes (ORS) 609.305).

Coyotes cannot be kept as a pet, ORS 610.045 and ORS 497.312. Coydogs would be under the authority of Oregon Dept. of Agriculture the same as hybrid wolves.

Pennsylvania: Species and subspecies of the coyote and a full-blooded wolf or crossbreed thereof not licensed by the Department of Agriculture.

Lawfully acquired coyotes may be imported or possessed, or both, by licensed propagators specifically for propagation for fur farming purposes. Coyotes imported under this exception and their progeny may not be sold or transferred for wildlife pet purposes or released into the wild. This subsection does not permit the sale for release or the release of the mammals into the wild. 34 PA. CONS. STAT. ANN. §2961 and §2963 58 Pa. Code §137.1.

Rhode Island: No person may possess, without first obtaining a permit from the department, animals of the following orders, families, and genera, Carnivores, Canidae, All persons obtaining a permit must demonstrate they have both adequate facilities, and adequate knowledge of animal health and husbandry to ensure both public safety and health. R.I. GEN. LAWS §4-18-3; 1994 R.I. PUB. LAWS 12 020 030

South Carolina: "Section 50-11-1765. (A) It is unlawful to sell live wolves or coyotes within the State or to possess, import, ship, or import live wolves or coyotes to be brought into this the State for personal possession. A person may not have a live wolf or coyote in his possession without a permit issued by the department or hybrid of either or both. For purposes of this section a hybrid wolf or hybrid coyote is an animal which is at least one-fourth wolf or coyote, or both."

South Dakota: A permit is required to possess any non-domestic mammal, or any hybrid thereof of the following orders: Carnivora (...Canidae — non-domestic) S.D. ADMIN. R. 12:68:18:03 and 12:68:18:03.01; and S.D. CODIFIED LAWS ANN. 40-14-2

Tennessee: "No wolves may be possessed without a permit, which includes very rigid pen specifications. Wolf hybrid of any percentage are not regulated by the Agency and are classified as Class III animals." TENN. CODE ANN §70-4-401, §70-4-403, and §70-4-404

Coyotes from a USDA licensed facility are allowed. Hybrids are not recognized.

Texas: No person may possess a dangerous wild animal without first obtaining a license (certificate of registration). Dangerous wild animals are defined as ... coyotes or hybrid. However, there are no requirements for a person possessing all other animals not listed above, such as wolves, etc. TEX. HEALTH & SAFETY CODE ANN. § 822.101-116; TEX. LOC. GOV'T CODE ANN. § 240.002(a) and § 240.0025

Utah: A person may not possess live zoological animals that are classified as prohibited. Prohibited animals include... the following families: ... Canidae (all species) ... However, in rare circumstances a person may possess these animals as a "pet" if the person obtains a certificate of registration from the Wildlife Board. UTAH ADMIN. R. 657-3-17, R. 657-3-24, R. 657-3-25, and R. 657-3-27

The Agricultural and Wildlife Damage Prevention Board, by authority granted under 4-23, declares it unlawful to import, distribute, relocate or possess live ... coyotes R58-14-3

Vermont: "A person shall not bring into, transport into, transport within, transport through, or possess in the State any live wild bird or animal of any kind without authorization from the Commissioner or his or her designee. VT. STAT. ANN. Tit. 10, §4709

Hybrids are considered domesticated

Virginia: Pure wolves are not allowed entrance into the state for private ownership. Hybrid wolves are no longer regulated by the Department of Game and Inland Fisheries, but per a mandate signed into law amending Chapter 918 of the Code of Virginia.

Any county, city or town may, by ordinance, establish a permit system to ensure the adequate confinement and responsible ownership of hybrid canines.

No person may possess nonnative exotic animals that are classed as predatory or undesirable as a "pet."

Washington: Washington Administrative Code (WAC) 220-450-030 prohibits the keeping of Washington wildlife in captivity without a permit from the Director. Though some exceptions apply, wanting to keep a species native to Washington as a pet would not be permitted. This WAC would prohibit both coyotes and wolves from being legal pets.

Hybrids are not considered wildlife and do not fall under WDFW's authority (WASH. REV. CODE §16-30). Domestic animals fall under the Department of Agriculture. City and county authorities can also further restrict what domestic animals are allowed in their areas of responsibility.

West Virginia: §20-2-13. No person shall transport into or have in his possession within this state any live wildlife...from without the state, except as authorized by an importation permit issued by the director: Provided, that the director shall not be authorized to issue a permit to any person to transport into this state any coyotes (*Canis latrans*). The Agency will also not issue a pet permit for coyote.

A person may not possess most dangerous non-native wild animals including gray wolves, hybrids, W. VA. CODE §19-34-1 to §19-34-9; W. VA. CODE R. §61-30-

Wisconsin: Wolves are listed as endangered species, so potential owners will need extra permitting from federal government. Wolf dogs and coyotes are listed as harmful wild animals and require a captive farm license. These are also subject to local ordinances. Coydogs have not been an issue, so there is no set regulation. Animals must be obtained from "captive" sources, not taken from the wild. All animals entering the state, even for a visit, must have permits from the Wisconsin Department of Agriculture.

Wyoming: Chapter 10, Section 5 (a) states: "Wolves (Canis lupus), wolf hybrids, and/or wolf/dog hybrids may not be imported or sold in the state of Wyoming." Predatory animals (except wolves and wolf hybrids) as defined in Wyoming Statute §23-1-101(a)(viii): coyote (*Canis latrans*) may be imported, possessed, transported, or confined without securing a permit from the Department.

US Territories and Protectorates: Importation of wolves, coyotes, dingoes, and hybrids is not permitted.

APPENDIX 2
Canada

Dingoes and dingo crosses are not legal for import. Some provinces or territories allow possession with permitting. HOWEVER, the permitting process is not guaranteed and may be extremely restrictive.

*** NOTE – Provincial laws are subject to change. Always confirm BEFORE bringing home a pure or cross wild canine. ***

Table 2: List of Canadian provinces and territories indicating the legality of owning wild canine, as of April 2019

	Wolf	Wolf cross	Coyote	Coydog
Alberta	No	Yes	No	Yes
British Columbia	No	No	No	No
Manitoba	No	No	No	No
New Brunswick	No	No	No	No
Newfoundland/ Labrador	Requires permit	Yes	Requires permit	Yes
Northwest Territories/ Nunavut	No	Yes	No	Check local ordinances
Nova Scotia	No	No	No	No
Ontario	Yes, but local restrictions apply	Yes, but local restrictions apply	Yes, but local restrictions apply	Yes, but local restrictions apply
Prince Edward Island	No	No	No	No
Quebec	Contact local authorities	Contact local authorities	Contact local authorities	Contact local authorities
Saskatchewan	Yes with provisions	Check municipal offices	Yes with provisions	Check municipal offices
Yukon	No	Contact local authorities	No	Contact local authorities

Alberta: Legislation does not prohibit a person from owning a hybrid of a wolf and a dog. Under provincial law, wolves are classified as furbearing animals and so cannot be kept as pets, but wolf/dog crosses can be legally possessed without special permits.

British Columbia: It is illegal to keep or sell a wolf or coyote or hybrid as a pet in BC.

Manitoba: In Manitoba it is illegal to "own" a wild animal. The Wildlife Act states that a wolf or coyote or any hybrid of either animal is considered a wild animal and therefore no person is allowed to "own" one. We provide permits to certain organizations such as the Assiniboine Zoo or our wildlife rehab centers in some cases for them to possess wild animals listed under The Wildlife Act.

A person will not be provided a permit to possess any wild animal in Manitoba except under very specific and rare circumstances.

Bringing (a wolf/hybrid) into Manitoba requires an import permit prior to entry being issued and generally we would not allow the import.

Ontario: Local restrictions apply for possession of pure or cross wolves or coyotes.

New Brunswick: Possession of wolves, coyotes, wolf-dog hybrids, or coyote-dog hybrids as pets is not permitted in New Brunswick.

Newfoundland and Labrador: The Dog Act specifies that a "dog" means a dog, male or female, and includes an animal which is a cross between a dog and a wolf; "fur bearing animal" means a... wolf or other animal that may be prescribed by regulation to be a fur bearing animal (including coyote).

Furbearer Management in Newfoundland and Labrador Eleven furbearer species are managed and trapped in Newfoundland and Labrador, including beaver, fox, lynx, coyote, mink, muskrat, otter, red squirrel, weasel, marten, and wolf.

Permits Required to Keep Live Wildlife "(E)very person in possession or control of live wildlife shall, immediately upon coming into that possession or control, apply in writing to the minister for a permit to keep the live wildlife in captivity" [WL Regs s.82]. However this requirement is avoided where a Ministerial license is held for "the taking or export of wild life for scientific purposes or for the purposes of propagation or for presentation to or exchange with an authority or body in another province of Canada or in another country" [WA s.7(3)].

Northwest Territories: "Dog" includes male and female dogs and an animal that is a cross between a dog and a wolf R.S.N.W.T. 1988, c. D-7, s. 167. No person shall capture, keep captive or possess live big game, fur-bearers, or other prescribed wildlife, unless such capture, captivity or possession is in accordance with the regulations or incidental to the legal harvest of the wildlife. Wildlife Act for the Northwest Territories

Nova Scotia: We do not permit hybrid coyotes in the province. Personal Pets Exotic Wildlife Prohibition List. Pursuant to Section 113 (1) (at) and (au) of the Wildlife Act, R.S.N.S. 1989, c504 and Section 6 of the General Wildlife Regulations, the Director of Wildlife has determined the following wildlife species or groups of wildlife species and their hybrids may not be kept as personal pets or imported into the province for use as personal pets:....3. All Canidae (except the domestic dog).

Prince Edward Island: It is illegal to own or possess wildlife on PEI without proper permits. Doing so can result in fines and/or legal costs.

Quebec: Despite numerous attempts, I was unable to get an answer from this province.

Saskatchewan: Before getting a wolf/dog cross, contact your municipal office as local bylaws may place restrictions on owning such pets.

Large carnivores are to be kept in an enclosure with a top or constructed in any other manner necessary to prevent escape over the fence and consisting of: (a) in the case of wolves... and coyotes, an area of not less than 200 square meters for up to two adult animals and an additional area of 20 square meters for each additional adult animal.

Yukon: Keeping wildlife in captivity 96(1) A person shall not keep live wildlife in captivity except under the authority of a license and in accordance with this Act. A person shall not import or transport live wildlife into the Yukon.

APPENDIX 3
Australia

According to the Australian Department of Environment and Energy, wolves and coyotes and their crosses may or may not be legally imported as pets. Check with the Australian Department of Environment and Energy before importing one.

It is illegal in Australia to remove a dingo from the wild and attempt to keep it as a pet. You can adopt one from a rescue.

For hybrid or otherwise non-pure dingoes, it is necessary to register with your local council.

*** NOTE: State laws are subject to change. Always confirm BEFORE bringing home a pure or cross wild canine. ***

Table 3: List of Australian states and territories indicating the legality of owning wild canines, as of April 2019. Also includes American territories in Oceania.

	Dingo	Dingo cross
ACT	Yes, with permit	Yes
New South Wales	Yes	yes
Northern Territory	Yes, with permit	Yes
Queensland	No	Contact local council
South Australia	Yes	Yes
Tasmania	No	No
Victoria	Yes, with license	Yes, with registry
Western Australia	Yes, with permit	Yes
US Territories in region	No	No

New South Wales: No permit required.

Queensland: Ownership of dingoes prohibited.

South Australia: Ownership of dingoes prohibited.

Tasmania: The dingo is a "restricted animal" under S32(1)(a)(a) of the Nature Conservation Act 2002 (The Act), and as such, it cannot be brought into the State without written permission of the Secretary of the Department:

"restricted animal means – (a) a fox, wolf, dingo and mink; and (c) a hybrid of an animal referred to in paragraph (a) or (b)."

This restriction applies to all movement, both permanent and temporary.

Additionally, the Act under S32(6) refer to the circumstances around which the Secretary may grant permission to import:

"(6) The Secretary may only grant permission under subsection (2) or (3) in respect of a restricted animal if the importation, possession or going at large of the restricted animal is required as part of a program to manage feral populations of animals of the same species as that restricted animal."

Victoria: Permit required from the Department of Sustainability and Environment. This also requires an escape-proof facility to safely house your dingo, of which must be a minimum size of 30 sq. meters, with a minimum fence height of 3 meters.

Western Australia: No permit required.

Northern Territory: Permit required.

Australian Capital Territory: Permit required.

www.ingramcontent.com/pod-product-compliance
Lightning Source LLC
Chambersburg PA
CBHW060044230426
43661CB00004B/644